Pathfinder
Indiana Life & Health Decoder & Workbook
INTRODUCTION

The **Decoder** section of this book is a valuable resource in your quest to pass the Indiana **State Law** portion of your examination to become a licensed L&H Producer. You will find all the information necessary to successfully answer the State Law questions which constitute **25%** of your exam.

The **Decoder** is a condensed and plain language version of Indiana insurance regulations which will direct your attention to the critical aspects of the laws that are tested. Keep in mind however, as a licensed Producer, staying current with insurance regulations is **your continuing responsibility** as insurance regulations change over time.

The **Workbook** portion of this book contains hundreds of practice quiz questions covering ALL subjects contained on the National and State sections of your exam. These quizzes are divided into **twelve** *National* chapter quizzes, **three** State Law quizzes, **two** Review quizzes, and **two** Final Exams. All quizzes and practice exams have been created by Pathfinder to give you a unique sense of how your *actual* licensing exam will look and feel with the same style and substance. Most Pathfinder students concur that questions in this workbook are actually more difficult than questions on the *actual* exam.

Please make certain you are thoroughly familiar with the State Law **Decoder** information presented at the beginning of this book, and that you have taken every quiz and practice exam **before** you take your *actual* exam. Doing so will give you the best chance of passing your State exam the first time! And…. that's what Pathfinder Pre-Licensing Courses are all about.

Pathfinder knows **our** success ultimately depends on **your** success!

Best of luck...
...The Pathfinder Team

TABLE OF CONTENTS

Section I - Indiana Law

Section 2 - Quizzes

Section 3 - L&H Exam Content Outline
See Black Stripe on book edge

LEGAL MILESTONES

A. Commerce Clause ... Paul vs Virginia

B. United States vs South Eastern Underwriters

C. McCarran Ferguson Act of 1945

INDIANA
GENERAL INSURANCE
LAWS, RULES & REGULATIONS

24 QUESTIONS

STUDY FOR EITHER L&H OR P&C LICENSE

The Department of Insurance

1   Most large industries are regulated primarily by the Federal Government, such as the communications, aviation and transportation industries. But the insurance industry is unique in that it is primarily regulated by **State Governments**. So the State of Indiana is primarily responsible for regulating the insurance industry in Indiana.

2   State Government works like the Federal Government in that there are three distinct branches of the government.

   A.   The Executive Branch **enforces** the law.

   B.   The Legislative Branch **creates** the law.

   C.   The Judicial Branch **interprets** the law.

3   The **Governor** is Indiana's Chief Executive Officer, and therefore is in charge of the State's Executive Branch of government. Hence the Governor is tasked with enforcing Indiana's insurance laws. Obviously, the Governor doesn't have the time to enforce insurance law, so **The Department of Insurance** was created by the Legislature to fulfill that function. The chief executive officer of the Indiana Department of Insurance (IDOI) is called the **Insurance Commissioner.**

© 2017 Pathfinder Corporation

The Insurance Commissioner

1 The Insurance Commissioner has the authority to **enforce State insurance law.** In addition, the Department of Insurance is given the power to supervise the organization, regulation, examination, rehabilitation, liquidation and conservation of all insurance companies doing business in the State of Indiana. The IDOI also supervises and regulates the licensing, education and examination of insurance Producers.

2 NOTE: As you study the law, please notice that almost all of the laws have been written to protect **the insuring public.** This is accomplished by making certain that the individuals and insurance Companies selling insurance in Indiana are properly trained, are financially solvent, act in ethical ways, and provide products that fulfill the Policyowners' needs at fair prices.

3 Because it is a rather complex job, the Commissioner has been granted limited powers from all three branches of government. The Commissioner has been granted:

A. **Executive Authority** to **enforce** State insurance law.

B. **Legislative Authority** to create **Rules** that explain or clarify laws.

C. **Judicial Authority** to hold **Administrative Hearings**.

Some Important Facts Concerning the Insurance Commissioner

A. The Commissioner is **appointed by the Governor (Gubernatorial Appointment)** and **serves at the pleasure** of the Governor. This means that the Governor may discharge the Commissioner at any time. There is no set term of office.

B. The Commissioner is selected solely on the basis of his or her **knowledge and skill** in insurance without regard to his or her political beliefs or affiliations.

C. The Commissioner must post a **bond** in the **sum of at least $50,000** to assure the faithful performance of his or her duties.

D. The Commissioner is authorized to participate in the **National Association of Insurance Commissioners (NAIC).**

The Commissioner's Duties Under the Law

1   The IDOI and the Commissioner have many important tasks under the law. We will address three major responsibilities of the Commissioner in this chapter.

> 1. *Assuring that insurance Companies meet basic standards.*
>
> 2. *Assuring that license Applicants meet the requirements to be licensed, and to maintain their licenses.*
>
> 3. *Assuring that Applicants, Producers and Companies adhere to both the Producer Licensing Law and the Unfair Competition Law.*

1. Assuring that Companies Meet Basic Standards

2   When a consumer purchases an insurance policy, they are actually purchasing a **promise** that their Insurance Company will pay any claims occurring in the future. Therefore, it is important to make certain that the Company is **fiscally (financially) healthy** enough to live up to its future promises. Hence, Indiana law requires that all Companies conducting business in this State must meet and maintain stringent financial standards. To understand this fully, you need to know more about the Companies that market insurance in Indiana and how they get permission (get admitted) to conduct business in Indiana.

Types of Companies based on their place of Origin (Where they started/Place of Domicile)

3   One way of classifying insurance Companies is by where they were **chartered or founded**. For example, was the Company started in Indiana, New York, or in London, England? How about New York Life, Mass Mutual or Mutual of Omaha? Or Sun Life of Toronto, or Lloyds of London?

1 Companies may be classified by **where they originated** into Domestic, Foreign or Alien.

1. **Domestic =** Chartered or formed in Indiana (Indiana Farmers).

2. **Foreign =** Chartered or formed in another state, territory or possession of the United States (New York Life).

3. **Alien =** Chartered or formed in another country (Lloyds of London).

Companies must be ADMITTED/AUTHORIZED

2 Before an insurance Company can do business in the State of Indiana, it must be **ADMITTED** by the Department of Insurance. The process of being admitted is very stringent in that it requires certain levels of capitalization, a sound business plan, a board of Directors and Officers that are of good character, etc.

3 Domestic Insurers will not be given a charter until they meet the State's minimum requirements. Foreign and Alien Insurers must demonstrate that they already meet those requirements. All Admitted Companies will be granted a **Certificate of Authority.**

4 A **Certificate of Authority** is to a Company what an **insurance license** is to a Producer.

5 Insurance Companies are granted Certificates of Authority. Producers are granted insurance licenses.

Some important enforcement tools that help assure companies meet fiscal/financial standards - Examination

A. The Commissioner **may examine** any Company doing business in Indiana at any time to ensure the Company is financially sound.

B. The Commissioner **must examine** all Companies doing business in Indiana at least **every 5 years. However,** in the case of Foreign or Alien Companies, if the Company's Home State complies with the NAIC Model Examination procedures, then the Indiana Commissioner may **waive** the Indiana examination and accept the Home State exam as adequate.

6 **Translation:** The Commissioner MUST examine all Domestic Companies every five years.

Rehabilitation and Liquidation

A. In a fiscal examination, the Commissioner examines the Company's books and records. Hopefully, the Commissioner will not find a problem. However, if during the examination the Commissioner finds something that would endanger the public (for example, the Company does not have enough money to pay claims), the Commissioner must give the Company **Notice** that there is a problem, and then conduct a **Hearing** to determine the extent of the problem. This procedure is called *Due Process*.

B. If after the hearing the Commissioner still finds the Company represents a risk to Indiana consumers, then the Commissioner may file for *Rehabilitation* in court.

C. The court-appointed Rehabilitators take over operation of the Company in an effort to save it. In the process, the stockholders, director and officers lose all of their powers and rights. Hopefully, the Rehabilitators will put the Company back on its feet. However...

D. If the Company cannot be made fiscally healthy (the rehabilitation doesn't work), the Commissioner has the authority to **liquidate the Company for the benefit of the Policyholders.**

Note #1: Policyholders and **Creditors** are not the same. The Creditors have **loaned** money to the Company, but the Company **owes claims** to the Policyowners. In the case of Liquidation, all **Policyowner claims** are paid first, not the corporate debt.

Note #2: The Commissioner has the authority to examine the books and records of any Producer or Agency at any time.

Note #3: The Law says that the Commissioner has the duty to **PROMULGATE** the laws to the Public, which means "to make the laws **KNOWN** to the Public".

Note #4: If the Commissioner finds that an Indiana domestic insurance company cannot pass the Indiana standard NAIC fiscal examination, then the Commissioner must report their findings to the NAIC.

Life & Health and Property & Casualty Guaranty Associations

1 Because the possibility exists that an Insurance Company may become insolvent/go bankrupt, the State Legislature has created the **Life & Health and Property & Casualty Guaranty Associations**. **All** Admitted Insurers must belong to the appropriate Association. The purpose of the Guaranty Associations is to protect the rights of Indiana Policyowners to their cash values, claim payments, death benefits, etc., contained in their insurance **policies.** Each company is assessed its pro rata share, and the State does NOT contribute any money (no tax dollars).

2 You should study the limits of liability for the appropriate Association for the license exam you are taking.

3 **LIFE & HEALTH** Should a L&H insurance Company go bankrupt, the Life and Health Guaranty Association pays the bankrupt Companies' **Policyowners** their policy benefits up to certain limits.

The maximum limits of liability of the **L&H Guaranty Association** are:

    A. $100,000 in **cash value** in either a Life Insurance policy or an Annuity.

    B. $300,000 in **death benefits** paid on the life of any one person.

    C. $300,000 in **Health claim benefits** per insured for a Health insurance policy.

4 **PROPERTY & CASUALTY** Should a P&C insurance Company become insolvent, the maximum limits of liability paid to the **Policyowners** by the P&C Guaranty Association are:

    A. $100,000 per claim.

    B. $300,000 per occurrence.

    C. For any claim for **return of unearned premium**, the Association will pay 80% of the unearned premiums paid, or $650 per month for up to a maximum of 12 months ($7,800), whichever is **LESS.**

2. Assuring that License Applicants/Producers Meet Certain Requirements

1   The second major responsibility of the Insurance Commissioner is that he/ she is tasked with protecting the consumers of the State by making certain that those individuals selling insurance (**Producers**) meet certain requirements plus demonstrate competency and honesty.

Important Information about Producer Licensing

2   You cannot act as an **Insurance Producer/Agent** unless you are licensed. It is important to note that the activities of an Insurance Producer, as defined by the law, are quite broad. The law says that anyone who "Acts or aids in any manner in **soliciting** applications for policies of insurance, or who **negotiates** a contract of insurance" must be licensed. The law does not allow an unlicensed individual to sell insurance, even if a Licensed Producer ultimately signs the application.

First, some DEFINITIONS

1. **A Person** is an individual, or a business entity (virtually anyone).

2. **An Insurance Producer** is a Person required to be licensed under the law to **sell, solicit, or negotiate** contracts of insurance.

3. **A Business Entity** is a corporation, partnership or association, which, for compensation, acts or aids in any manner in soliciting applications for a policy of insurance or in negotiating a policy of insurance on behalf of an Insurer. The Business Entity (insurance **Agency**) itself must be licensed, and it must appoint a licensed Producer as its **Licensed Compliance Officer** who is responsible for making certain that the Business Entity/Agency and all of its Producers comply with the insurance laws.

4. **A License** is the document issued by the Commissioner which authorizes a person to act as an Insurance Producer for the line or lines of authority specified on the license, such as Life, Health or Property & Casualty.

© 2017 Pathfinder Corporation

The Producer must also be **APPOINTED** by an Insurer. This is done by the Producer entering into a contractual relationship with each Insurance Company that the Producer represents. This contractual relationship, called an **Agency Agreement or Agency Appointment**, makes the Producer a legal **AGENT** of the Insurance Company. **Agents legally represent Companies**, and are legal extensions of those Companies. Remember: You are LICENSED by the State, and APPOINTED by your insurance company.

5. **Sell** means to exchange a contract of insurance for money.

6. **Solicit** means attempting to sell, or urging a person to apply for an insurance policy.

7. **Negotiate** is the act of conferring directly with, or offering advice to a purchaser, or prospective purchaser, about an insurance contract/policy.

Types of Licenses

There are seven types of licenses we will address in this chapter. They are:
1. Resident Producer
2. Non-Resident Producer
3. Temporary
4. Consultant
5. Limited Lines
6. Surplus Lines (P&C only)
7. Independent Adjuster

1. Resident Producer License Specifics

A **Resident** Producer license allows an individual or business entity to sell Life and/or Health Insurance, or Property and Casualty Insurance in Indiana. A Life & Health license does NOT authorize you to sell P&C insurance, or vice versa.

You may only be a Resident of **ONE STATE AT A TIME**, and therefore you may only hold a **Resident** Producer license in **one State at a time**. So if you are a **Resident** Producer in Indiana, and you wish to sell in other States, you will need to get Non-Resident licenses in those other States.

There are specific requirements that must be met in order to hold a Resident Producer License in the State of Indiana.

© 2017 Pathfinder Corporation

Indiana Resident Producer License Requirements: You must

A. Either **live** in Indiana, or have your **primary place of business** in Indiana.

B. Be at least age 18.

C. Complete a mandatory prelicensing course of instruction (with a few exceptions). The Course Provider will issue to you a **Certificate of Completion** which is essentially your ticket to take your examination. Place the Certificate in your valuable papers file once you have completed your licensing process.

   BE ADVISED: **YOUR CERTIFICATE OF COMPLETION IS ONLY GOOD FOR SIX (6) MONTHS!** If you have not passed your exam **and** submitted an Application for a license to the IDOI **within SIX months**, you will need to take the prelicensing course again! Don't let this happen to you!

D. Pass the State exam. The exams are administered by Ivy Tech.

E. Submit a license application (NAIC Uniform Application) to the IDOI.

F. Pay the licensing fees.

G. Be deemed by the Commissioner to be **competent, trustworthy, financially responsible,** and have a good personal and business reputation.

Exam Exceptions:

Certain individuals in certain circumstances are exempt from taking the exam, either in whole or in part. The first group is people who have **advanced designations** in **Life** insurance. The second group is people who have advanced designations in **Property & Casualty**. The third group is people who already have Producer licenses in other States, who now wish to **move to Indiana** and obtain an Indiana Producer license.

A. **LIFE -** Individuals who have obtained the designation of Chartered Life Underwriter (CLU), Certified Financial Planner (CFP) or Chartered Financial Consultant (ChFC) and apply for a Life insurance Producer license, will only be required to take the Indiana State law portion of the exam.

   CLU   CFP   ChFC

© 2017 Pathfinder Corporation

B. **PROPERTY & CASUALTY -** Individuals who have obtained the designation of Chartered Property Casualty Underwriter (CPCU), Certified Insurance Counselor (CIC), or Accredited Advisor in Insurance (AAI) and apply for a Property and Casualty Producer license, will only be required to take the Indiana State law portion of the exam.

CPCU   CIC   AAI

C. **MOVING FROM ANOTHER STATE -** Individuals who are Resident Producers in another state and who move to Indiana and wish to obtain an Indiana Resident Producer license must surrender their license to the State which granted it, **and apply for an Indiana license within 90 days.** If they do so, **no exam** will be required.

A Producer living in another State wanting to sell in Indiana would need to be granted an Indiana Non-Resident license, which is the next license.

2. <u>Non-Resident Producer License Specifics</u>

A **Non-Resident** Producer License is issued to Producers **from other States** who want to sell insurance in Indiana. For example, if a Licensed Michigan Resident Producer has the opportunity to sell policies to customers in Indiana, then the Michigan Producer would need to apply for an Indiana **Non-Resident** Producer License. An Agent may hold multiple NON-RESIDENT licenses, but may only hold one ONE RESIDENT Agent's license at a time. There are some specific requirements to hold a Non-Resident Producer License in Indiana.

Non-Resident Producer License Requirements: An individual must:

A. Be licensed as a Resident Producer in another State, and be in good standing in their home state.

B. Complete the NAIC Uniform Non-Resident Producer License application.

C. Pay the required Indiana Non-Resident licensing fees.

Please note: **No exam** is required to obtain a Non-Resident Producer license if the State where the Applicant is licensed and Indiana have **reciprocity**. Reciprocity means that Indiana and another State agree to have the same requirements for a Producer to receive a Non-Resident license. Most States now have reciprocity with all other States. This makes it extremely easy for you to obtain Non-Resident Producer Licenses in other States.

© 2017 Pathfinder Corporation

3. Temporary Producer License Specifics

A **Temporary** Producer License may be issued by the Commissioner, **without an examination**, in certain **hardship** circumstances, such as the **death, disability or** military **deployment** of a licensed Producer (three **D's**). The Commissioner essentially allows a person who is close to the situation to temporarily act as a Producer, with certain restrictions, in order to continue the *real* Producer's business. The reason for the granting of a Temporary license is to better serve the Producer's Policyholders.

1

A Temporary Producer License is good for up to 180 days.

The holder of a Temporary Producer License can **service** the *existing* **business** of the absent Resident Producer, but they **cannot solicit** *new* **business!**

2

A Temporary Producer License may be granted as follows:

A. **DEATH** – To the spouse of a **deceased** Producer, or to an executor of deceased Producer's estate.

B. **DISABILITY** – To the spouse, employee or guardian of a **disabled** Resident Producer.

C. **DEPLOYED** – To an individual designated by the Resident Producer in the event the Producer is **deployed** in the military.

D. **PUBLIC INTEREST** – To any individual under other circumstances in which the Commissioner feels that granting of a Temporary license serves the public interest.

Restrictions on the activities of a Temporary License Holder

Temporary License Holders are restricted to:

A. **Servicing** existing accounts

B. **Training** personnel

C. **Selling** the business

Again, Temporary License Holders **may not sell or solicit new business!**

© 2017 Pathfinder Corporation

4. Insurance Consultant License Specifics : Fee Based

1   Insurance **Consultants** are individuals who are licensed to **sell insurance advice for a fee.** They may **NOT sell insurance for a commission**, or receive any part of a commission for their services.

2   A licensed Producer **cannot also be licensed as a Consultant**, because no person can hold both licenses at the same time.

3   A Producer, however, **can ACT as a Consultant**. To **ACT** as a Consultant, a Producer must fill out the proper consultation forms and have them signed by the client **prior** to the time that the transaction occurs. A Producer may even accept **both a fee and a commission** in the same transaction, **if full disclosure** is made about the compensation arrangements, again, prior to the time that the transaction occurs.

4   Attorneys, trust officers of banks, and a very few others are exempt from needing to be licensed as insurance Consultants in order to provide insurance advise for a fee.

5. Limited Lines Producer License Specifics

5   A **Limited Lines Insurance Producer** is an individual or corporation that is authorized by the Commissioner to solicit **specialty insurance products.**

6   The Commissioner *may* issue a **Limited Producer** license to individuals in the categories listed below **without requiring an examination.** The exceptions to the NO EXAM rule are the **Funeral Directors**, who must take the Life Producer exam, and applicants wanting to sell only **Crop – Hail** insurance who must take the P&C Producers exam.

The following persons must hold a **Limited Producer** license:

A. **TRAVEL** – A person selling Limited Travel Accident insurance (for example, *Flight* insurance) in transportation terminals. No pre-licensing study, no exam, and no Continuing Education (CE) are required.

B. **PORTABLE ELECTRONICS** – Battery-operated portable electronic devices, such as cell phones, portable/laptop computers, digital cameras, pagers, GPS, listening devices, and gaming systems.

© 2017 Pathfinder Corporation

Insurance for portable electronic devices is normally offered at the point-of-sale in retail electronics stores. The store itself must be licensed to offer the insurance. The coverage is for repair or replacement of the portable electronic device. Covered perils typically include loss, damage. or mechanical breakdown.

C. **BAGGAGE** – A ticket selling agent of a common carrier who issues insurance on the personal effects (*Baggage* insurance for your "stuff") in connection with the transportation provided by that carrier. No pre-licensing study, no exam, and no Continuing Education are required.

D. **TITLE** – A person selling *Title* insurance. Title insurance is insurance that is normally obtained in real estate transactions to indemnify the purchaser of the property against loss resulting from a defect in the title to the property. For example, existing tax liens against the property. Applicants must take 10 hours of pre-licensing study, but no exam is required. However, license holders must complete 7 hours of CE every two years.

E. **CREDIT** – A person selling *Credit Life* or *Credit Health* insurance. This is the type of insurance you might purchase from a lending institution in connection with a debt (borrowing money), such as a mortgage on a home. For example, *Mortgage Protection* insurance. Applicants must complete a special course of study in order to obtain the license, but no exam and no CE are required.

F. **FUNERAL DIRECTORS / PRE - NEED** – Funeral Directors may obtain a Limited Life insurance license to sell **pre-need funeral expense policies** (Life insurance to cover the cost of the funeral). These individuals must complete the standard Life insurance prelicensing course and pass the regular Life Producer examination, but their business is **limited** to the sale of Life insurance associated with their Pre-Need business. Funeral Directors must complete a one-time 10 hour continuing education course after obtaining their life insurance license. Thereafter, there are no further continuing education requirements for Funeral Directors.

G. **CROP - HAIL** – P&C licensed Producers may sell Crop - Hail insurance. However, individuals who want to **sell ONLY Crop – Hail** insurance, must first obtain the full P&C Producers license, and then downgrade their license to a **Limited Lines Crop – Hail license**. In that case, **only 5 hours** of CE is required every two years (instead of the normal 20 hours).

6. Surplus Lines License (Property & Casualty Only)

1

Surplus Lines Producers represent **Non-Admitted** insurance Companies, i.e. those Companies who have chosen **not** to obtain permission to market insurance in Indiana. For example, a Company that sells only off-shore drilling rig insurance probably sees no need for its products in a State like Indiana, which has no off-shore oil business.
The Surplus Lines business is unique in that it provides access to many specialty coverages that otherwise would not be available in the State, such as Life insurance for race horses, coverage for special events such as the Indy 500 race, or liability coverage for a traveling circus.

2

Surplus Lines Applicants must first obtain a Property & Casualty license. Then they must pass the Surplus Lines exam, file the appropriate application and pay the licensing fees.

3

One of the most unique features of Surplus Lines Producers is that they must **collect a gross premium tax of 2½%** on the policies they sell, and pay the money to the IDOI twice per year. The reason why the Surplus Lines Producer must collect the tax is the IDOI cannot tax the Companies because they are **Non-Admitted**.

4

Surplus Lines Producers MUST make a diligent effort to place all of their *Surplus Lines* business with Admitted Insurers **before** they go to the Surplus Lines markets. **The Surplus Lines markets may NOT used just to obtain lower premium rates**.

5

Surplus Lines Producers will share commissions with *normal* P&C Producers who bring Surplus Lines business to them.

6

Surplus Lines licenses will renew at the same time as the Producer's P&C license.

7. Independent Adjuster License

All of the above categories of insurance licenses (except Consultants) are for individuals that **sell, solicit, or negotiate** contracts of insurance. The Independent Adjuster License is very different, because it is for individuals that **adjust claims**, as opposed to individuals that sell insurance.

Obtaining and Maintaining a License: Continuing Education Requirements, License Renewal and More

1 A Producer license remains in effect, unless suspended or revoked, as long as the renewal fees are paid and the Continuing Education requirements are met by the Producer.

Continuing Education = CE

2 Insurance Producer licenses must be **RENEWED every two (2) years**.

3 A total of **24 hours of Continuing Education** must be obtained during the two year period in order to renew a Producer license. The 24 hour requirement holds true regardless of the number of lines of authority a Producer has, such as both a Life & Health and a Property & Casualty. You will still only need 24 hours of CE, and it could be all L&H or all P&C, or a mixture.

4 Excess Continuing Education hours may not be carried over to the next renewal period.

PRODUCERS: TWENTY FOUR HOURS EVERY TWO YEARS: 24 IN 2

Again, the CE requirements for the various licenses are:

A.	TRAVEL	0
B.	PORTABLE ELECTRONICS	0
C.	BAGGAGE	0
D.	TITLE	7
E.	CREDIT	0
F.	FUNERAL DIRECTORS	0
G.	CROP – HAIL	5
H.	LIFE ONLY	24
I.	HEALTH ONLY	24
J.	LIFE & HEALTH	24
K.	PROPERTY & CASUALTY	24
L.	L&H + P&C	24
M.	P&C + SURPLUS LINES	24
N.	INDEPENDENT ADJUSTER	24

WHAT HAPPENS IF YOU LET YOUR LICENSE LAPSE?

REINSTATEMENT

Producers who allow their license to lapse will face sanctions as follows:

A. If a Producer has allowed a license to lapse **within the past 12 months, but HAD COMPLETED all of their required Continuing Education BEFORE THEIR LICENSE RENEWAL DATE, they may reinstate their license by paying a reinstatement penalty of 3 times (3X) the usual license renewal fee,** plus their normal license renewal fee. The Commissioner may waive the penalty if the **license lapsed within the past 30 days.** No test required.

B. Producers who have allowed their license to lapse within the past 12 months, but who **did NOT complete** their CE requirements before the license renewal date, MUST do the following to **REINSTATE** their license:

   1. Complete their CE requirements.

   2. Pay the 3x reinstatement penalty as stated above.

   3. Take and pass the State Regulations section of the Producers licensing exam.

   4. Pay the normal license renewal fee.

C. Producers who have let their license lapse for **more than twelve (12) months** must start the licensing process all over again!

Notice the penalties imposed if you fail to get your CE completed BEFORE the end of your two (2) year licensing cycle!!! **BEWARE!**

STAYING IN TOUCH/CHANGE OF ADDRESS & *THE 30 DAY RULE*

All Producers must notify the Commissioner **within 30 days** of any change of residential, business address, or email address. Failure to do so requires a **mandatory penalty/ fine of $100**, and is grounds for losing your license. *Change of Address* is now easily accomplished by entering into your Producer account in the SIRCON database through the Pathfinder web site at **www. PathFinderEdu.com**

BULLETIN 177: PAYMENT OF AGENT COMMISSIONS, COMMISSION SPLITTING, REFERRAL FEES, AND REBATING

1. Commissions may only be paid to licensed persons, who are called **Producers.**

2. Commissions may NOT be paid to unlicensed persons.

3. Persons who are not licensed shall not accept commissions.

4. Licensed Producers **may share commissions** with other Producers.

   However, in the event that **only one** of the Producers has the proper qualifications to make the sale, a commission or referral fee **can still be shared** with the nonqualified Producer as long as the nonqualified Producer **does not participate** in the sale, solicitation, or negotiation.

5. Licensed Producers may pay a **referral fee/Finder's Fee** to a non-licensed person as long as that person **does not participate** in the sale, solicitation, or negotiation of insurance. Also, the payment of a referral fee to a non-licensed person **must NOT be conditioned** on the purchase of insurance, nor may the dollar amount of any purchase be a factor in determining the amount of the referral fee paid to the non-licensed person.

   Translation: Producers pay *referral fees* for **leads, not sales.**

6. Licensed Producers **may not give part of their commission**, or anything of value, not specifically stated in the insurance policy, back to a client in order to induce that client to purchase insurance from the Producer. Doing so is called **REBATING.**

   Giving something of value to a client that is not specifically stated in the contract is an illegal practice known as *REBATING* which is a criminal offense. **REBATE = JAILBAIT.**

   Gifts to a client of any value are prohibited if the gift is an inducement to, or conditioned upon, the purchase of renewal of insurance.

7. A Producer may assign their commissions to an insurance Agency, if that Agency/Business entity is also licensed. And all Agencies must be licensed as *Producers* (obviously no test required).

CONTROLLED BUSINESS

The Controlled Business law is designed to keep a person from obtaining an insurance license **primarily for the purpose of purchasing their own**

insurance at a discount. A person who needs large amounts of insurance coverages, say for business reasons, could obtain an insurance license and get substantial savings by receiving the commissions on their own purchases. The purpose of the Controlled Business law is to prevent people who have no intent of selling insurance to others, from keeping a license just to buy their own insurance for less money.

Controlled Business is defined as insurance written by Producers on:

1. Themselves.

2. Their immediate family.

3. Their employer or employees.

4. Anyone else on whom they exert a significant amount of influence.

Writing business on **your friends** is NOT considered Controlled Business.

Controlled Business is **not prohibited, but limited** by statute not to exceed **25% of your commission income, earned in any 12 month period of time.**

3. Assuring Applicants, Producers and Companies adhere to the Producer Licensing Laws and the Unfair Competition Laws

1 The third major responsibility of the Insurance Commissioner is the enforcement of the Producer Licensing Law and the Unfair Competition/ Unfair Trade Practices Law. The focus of both laws is, of course, **to protect the citizens of Indiana**. The Producer Licensing law seeks to ensure that licensed Producers are **competent and trustworthy**, while the Unfair Competition Law endeavors to regulate insurance business practices for the benefit of Indiana Policyowners and citizens.

Producer Licensing Law

2 The Producer Licensing Law provides a laundry list of acts which are violations of the law. It also sets out procedures for dealing with violations and sets parameters for the discipline to be imposed by the Commissioner. The statute also addresses sanctions which may be imposed if a Producer is in arrears/delinquent in court-ordered child support payments.

Violations Under the law

The following is a list of violations that you as a Producer may not do. Common sense would tell you that all this stuff is illegal. If it sounds bad, it is bad, and therefore illegal.

1. **Cheating** on your licensing examination.

2. Making material **misstatements** on your license application.

3. Obtaining, or attempting to obtain, a license through misrepresentation or **fraud**.

4. Having a Producer license suspended or **revoked** in another state.

5. Any cause for which issuance of your license could have been refused had it been known to the Commissioner at the time of license issuance.

6. **Misrepresenting** of the terms of any insurance policy.

7. **Forging** another's name to an application for insurance.

8. **Violating** of any insurance laws or violation of any lawful rule, regulation or order of the Indiana Commissioner, or of the Commissioner of another state.

9. **Breach of fiduciary duty** (example: misappropriating funds/stealing the premiums).

10. Using fraudulent, coercive or dishonest practices; demonstrating incompetence, **untrustworthiness**, financial irresponsibility, or not performing in the best interest of the insuring public.

11. Lying during the replacement of an existing insurance policy. This is referred to as **Twisting**.

12. Being found guilty of any Unfair Trade Practice.

13. Being **convicted** of a felony.

14. Failing to pay State income tax.

15. Failing to complete your Continuing Education requirements.

16. Knowingly accepting insurance business from someone who is not licensed.

17. **Failing to notify** the Commissioner of a change in legal name or address. In the case of *Change of Address*, a Producer has **30 days** to notify the Commissioner.

18. **Failure to pay child support.** An Insurance Producer who is delinquent in court-ordered child support payments is in danger of losing his or her license. In this regard the law defines *delinquent* as either more than **$2000**, or **three months** in arrears. There are essentially two avenues for *child support* licensing sanctions.

   A. The **Court** who has jurisdiction over the support and custody matters can order that the Producer's license be suspended. The Court notifies the Commissioner, who in turn notifies the Producer. The suspension automatically begins **5 days** after the Commissioner sends *Notice of Suspension* to the Producer's address of record. Appeals of this type of suspension must be made to the Court of Original Jurisdiction, and not the Commissioner.

   B. Should the **State** have had to provide assistance to the children in lieu of child support, the agency rendering that assistance shall notify the Commissioner of the delinquent child support payments. The Commissioner shall automatically place the Producer on probation. The *Probation Notice* shall inform the Producer of how to "take care" of the problem, e.g., payment in full, set up a payment schedule, or set up a withholding plan, etc. Should the agency notify the Commissioner that the Producer has not "taken care of" the arrearage/delinquency; the Commissioner shall immediately suspend the Producer's license. Under the statute the entire process shall be completed within **20 days** of the Commissioner's initial mailing to the Producer.

NOTE: A Business Entity (insurance **Agency**) can also have its license suspended or revoked if its **Licensed Compliance Officer**:

Fails to report a suspected law violation to the Commissioner, **and no corrective action is taken.**

© 2017 Pathfinder Corporation

Procedures the Commissioner Follows in Connection with Licensing Law Violations

1 The Commissioner will **notify** the Applicant or Licensee/Producer by regular first class mail that their application for a license or their request for renewal has been denied.

2 The Applicant or Licensee/Producer has **63 days from the date the notice** was mailed to make a written demand for a hearing. The hearing must be **held within 30 days after the request** is made.

If, after a hearing, the Commissioner finds a violation has occurred, the Commissioner may:

    A. **Censure** a Producer (disapproval).

    B. Issue a **letter of reprimand**.

    C. Place a Producer on **probation**, and require regular reports, remedial education, or limit the type of business the Producer can solicit/write.

    D. Order the Producer to **make restitution** (pay back what was stolen).

    E. Impose a civil **fine** of not less than $50, nor more than $10,000 per violation.

    F. The Commissioner may also *permanently revoke* an insurance Producer's license.
      "Permanently revoked" means that:
      (1) The Producer's license shall **never** be reinstated; and
      (2) The former licensee is **not eligible** to submit an application for a new license.

Because the Commissioner **must notify all appointing insurance Companies** of a Producer Licensing Law violation, the Commissioner will:

    A. Request the Producer **provide a list** of all appointing Insurers. If such a request is made, the Producer has **10 days** to supply the list to the Commissioner. If the Producer does not respond within 10 days, the Commissioner, in addition to any previous sanctions, may suspend the Producer's license **without a hearing.**

    B. The Commissioner must then notify all appointing Insurers of the suspension or revocation of the Producer's license.

© 2017 Pathfinder Corporation

Unfair Competition Law/Unfair Trade Practices

The Unfair Competition Law, also known as the Unfair Trade Practices Act, is the **Golden Rule** of the Insurance business. What it basically says is that everybody, the Consumer, other Producers and other insurance Companies, shall be given a fair shake. If you don't want something done to you, don't do it to someone else!

Violations under the Law

1. A Producer may not **misrepresent the terms of a policy** to be sold in this state.

2. A Producer may not make an **untrue, deceptive or misleading statement** about any person engaged in the insurance business.

3. A Producer may not make a **false, derogatory or maliciously critical statement** about the financial condition of an insurance Company which is calculated to hurt anyone in the insurance business.

4. A Producer may not **restrain trade;** i.e., obstruct the normal business process of insurance.

5. A Producer may not circulate any **false statement about the financial condition** of any Insurance Company with the intent to deceive the public. That means your Company, the other guy's Company, or any Company. No *badmouthing*!

6. A Producer **may not offer anything of value to a prospective buyer that is not specified in the policy as an <u>inducement</u> to buy insurance from them**. A Producer may not give stock, benefit certificates, or contracts as an <u>inducement</u> to buy insurance. Again, this is **REBATING** which is **an illegal inducement.**

7. A **gift** that is meant to induce the purchase of insurance is against the law. However, promotional items (for instance, those given with a quote) which have a Fair Market Value of **$25** or less are acceptable so long as the gift is not given on condition of the sale of a policy.

© 2017 Pathfinder Corporation

8. Neither the Producer nor their Company may write or issue any policy or contract that **unfairly discriminates** between individuals of the **SAME** insuring class. Policyowners in the same insuring class should all be paying the same premium rates.

9. A lending institution *may not require* that a borrower insure mortgaged property by **purchasing insurance** *from the lending institution as a condition for obtaining a mortgage.* However, it **may** require that property be insured, and can exercise right of approval over the Insurer selected. The same principle applies to the contract sale of real estate. Like a mortgage lender, the contract seller can insist upon adequate insurance.

10. A Producer may not enter into a conspiracy to **restrain trade** in the business of insurance.

11. A Producer may not **monopolize** or conspire with others to monopolize any part of the insurance business. (However, membership in a Not For Profit Trade Association of Producers, or other insurance groups, shall not in itself constitute restraint of trade.)

12. A Producer may not discriminate financially against an individual solely because of **blindness or partial blindness** unless the refusal is based on actuarial principles.

13. A Producer may not commit or perform **unfair claim settlement practices.**

14. A Producer may not unilaterally **cancel** an individual's Health coverage solely because of a change in the individual's medical condition.

15. A Producer may not use unlicensed persons to act as Producers.

NOTE: *Although these are some of the most important activities that are considered to be violations of the law, this is not a complete list. Over time, the Legislature has classified certain marketing and underwriting practices as violations of this law.*

Producers should always keep up-to-date on any statutory guidelines regarding those particular policies that they sell.

Unfair Claim Settlement Practices Law

The Unfair Claim Settlement Practice law is designed to ensure that claims are paid in a timely and fair manner. Again, if it sounds unfair, it is illegal!

Violations under the Law

A Company or its Producers may **not**:

1. Fail to acknowledge and act promptly on claims.

2. Refuse to pay claims without a reasonable investigation.

3. Fail to acknowledge claim coverage within a reasonable time after submission of proof of loss.

4. Fail to attempt to promptly and fairly settle claims in which liability is clear.

5. Offer the Insured substantially less than what a lawsuit would award, forcing litigation.

6. Attempt to settle a claim for less than the amount the Claimant would have believed he was entitled to as a result of Company advertising.

7. Attempt to settle a claim based on an application which was altered by the Producer or Company without notice to or consent of the Insured.

8. Make claim payments which are not accompanied by a statement containing the coverage under which the payments are being made.

9. Disclose a history of appealing arbitrated decisions in order to threaten the Claimant into accepting less than the settlement awarded.

10. Delay the investigation or paying of a claim by requiring the Claimant to submit multiples of the same information.

11. Fail to promptly settle claims (where liability is reasonably clear) under one section of the policy coverage in order to influence settlements under other sections.

© 2017 Pathfinder Corporation

12. Fail to promptly explain the denial of a claim or an offer of compromise in relation to the facts and applicable law.

13. Fail to use reasonable standards in the prompt investigation of claims.

14. Consistently assign some percentage of fault to an injured person seeking to recover from an injury despite the obvious absence of fault.

Investigation and Resolution of Unfair Claim Practice Complaints

1   Persons who feel that they have been victimized by a claims practice which they believe to be unfair may file a complaint with the Commissioner.

Within **10 business days**, the **Commissioner** shall:

1. Send a copy of the complaint to the Company involved.

2. Inform the complaining party in writing of the action taken by the Department, as well as any further action which might be contemplated.

Within **20 business days**, the Company shall, after a prompt and thorough
2   investigation, provide to the Commissioner and the complaining party, a written report stating:

1. The specific reasons for its action, or lack thereof.

2. A good faith estimate as to when the claim will be settled.

Annually, the Commissioner publishes reports of valid consumer complaints.
3   Each Company is evaluated based upon the number of valid complaints, in light of the premium dollars earned in Indiana.

Enforcement of Unfair Competition and Unfair Claim Practice Law

1   If the Commissioner believes that a Producer has engaged in an unfair trade practice, a **Hearing** will be held. The Producer will be given **Notice** of the charges at least **five days** in advance of the Hearing.

*NOTE: **Notice** and **Hearing** = **Due Process***.

2   If the Hearing involves a complaint made by an individual who is not an employee of the Department of Insurance, a copy (in substance) of the complaint must be attached to the Notice.

3   If you are the Producer, you have the right to tell your side of the story, i.e., present evidence, cross-examine witnesses and be represented by Counsel.

4   At the Hearing, the Commissioner may subpoena and examine witnesses and records.

5   If anyone fails to comply with the Commissioner's subpoena, the Commissioner may have a subpoena enforced by a Court.

6   A copy of charges, all evidence submitted, and the testimony given will be incorporated as the record of the proceedings. The Commissioner will make an informal finding of the facts based upon this Hearing as recorded in the transcript.

7   The Commissioner can order the Producer to stop doing whatever it was that caused the trouble in the first place, i.e., **cease and desist**.

8   When the Commissioner (a member of the Executive branch of the government) imposes fines, he or she is acting like a Judge. The American system of government embodies the principle of "separation of powers".

Judicial Review

Thus, when the Commissioner starts acting like a Judge, the Producer has the right to request a real Judge review the Commissioner's decision. This is called **Judicial Review**. Findings made and any penalties imposed by the Commissioner in regard to violations of the Unfair Competition Act may be appealed to the proper Court much like any other civil lawsuit.

Penalties for Violation of the Unfair Competition Law

UN-KNOWING VIOLATIONS - In addition to issuing the Cease-and-Desist order, the Commissioner may subject a Producer up to a **$25,000** fine per violation. This may not exceed an aggregate total penalty of **$100,000** in any 12-month period.

$25K to $100K

KNOWING VIOLATIONS - However, if the Producer knew, or reasonably should have known, that they were violating the law, the penalty may be up to **$50,000** per violation, not to exceed an aggregate total of **$250,000** in any 12 months. The Commissioner may also suspend or revoke the Producer's license.

$50K to $250K

VIOLATING A CEASE-AND-DESIST ORDER - If the Producer continues the activities **in violation of the Cease-and-Desist order,** the Producer is subject to a fine of up to **$25,000** per violation, and suspension or revocation of his or her license. A Company that violates a Cease-and-Desist order is subject to the same fine *and* suspension of its Certificate of Authority.

PLUS $25K

NOTE: The Commissioner **can only impose civil penalties.** The Commissioner **has no criminal authority at all (can NOT put you in jail).** However, if the Commissioner feels a criminal violation has occurred, the Commissioner may choose to hand the records of the case over to the county prosecutor who may then seek criminal penalties.

Criminal Penalties for Reckless Violators: A YEAR IN JAIL

1   Reckless violations of the Indiana Insurance Code are crimes, punishable as Class A Misdemeanors, which are punishable by fines not to exceed $5,000 and **up to 365 days in jail.**

The Fraudulent Claims Statute

2   Fraudulent insurance claims are estimated to cost the insurance industry billions of dollars per year. Their increased costs are passed along to the consumer in the form of higher premiums.

3   The Fraudulent Claims Statute exists to further the public policy in reducing insurance fraud.

4   The Fraudulent Claims Statute requires that all **claim forms** provided by an Insurer to a Claimant must contain the following **statement**:

5   *"A person who knowingly and with intent to defraud an Insurer, files a statement of claim containing any false, incomplete, or misleading information commits a felony."*

Whistle Blower's Immunity

6   Any person who in good faith reports a suspected insurance fraud to law enforcement officials, the Commissioner or the NAIC, shall be immune from any civil liability for damages.

© 2017 Pathfinder Corporation

INDIANA
LIFE LAWS, RULES &
REGULATIONS

8 Questions

1. <u>EMPLOYERS HAVE AN INSURABLE INTEREST IN THEIR EMPLOYEES</u>

1 By Indiana statute/law, Employers have an **insurable interest** in the lives and health of their employees.

2 Therefore, an Employer may purchase life/health insurance policies on their Employees (example: Key Employee Life or Key Employee Health). However, the Employer must provide written notice to the Employee. The Employee must object to the purchase of the insurance within 30 days of the notice. Otherwise, it will be presumed that the Employee has granted consent to the Employer for the purchase.

2. <u>NOTE TO STUDENTS: Understanding The Difference Between "Rules" and "Laws"</u>

3 **Laws** are written by the Indiana General Assembly, and are signed into law by the Governor. Most of what you are studying in this State Law Decoder are Laws. However, the Commissioner at times needs to explain/interpret or expand upon a law. The Commissioner's interpretations are called *"RULES"* or *"REGULATIONS"*.

4 Rules are explanations of a statute/law. In Indiana, Rules carry the same force and effect as the statute/law that they are designed to explain.

5 This **Decoder** gives you the **Rule** numbers, but the numbers themselves are NOT tested. Just know the information contained in the **Rules**.

3. UNDERWRITING RESTRICTIONS: AIDS & HIV-Rule 39

1 Insurance Companies can use HIV and AIDS as factors **in life and health** underwriting, but how the information is collected, the testing methods and the sharing of information with others are all regulated by law.

A. Collection of Information

2 Questions on an application for Life or Health insurance can seek medically specific information regarding AIDS and HIV. However, **no** information may be sought, either directly or indirectly, concerning an Applicant's sexual orientation.

B. AIDS Testing

3 Insurance Companies may, at their own expense, require AIDS testing.

4 All Applicants must give their written permission for AIDS testing, and the results must be kept confidential.

5 The Company may report test results to the MIB, but the presence of HIV may NOT be revealed to the MIB. However, the Company may indicate to the MIB that the individual had "abnormal test results."

6 Companies **cannot** use the fact that an Applicant sought AIDS testing or counseling in the past as an underwriting tool to rate the Applicant or deny coverage.

C. Benefit to the Insured of Being Asked AIDS Questions

7 Once the Policyowner/Insured has been accepted by the Company, the policy can NOT exclude AIDS related losses, nor may benefits be reduced for AIDS related claims.

8 **Remember:** There is no law requiring a Company to accept an AIDS risk, but once an AIDS Applicant has been accepted, there can be no policy exclusion for AIDS.

© 2017 Pathfinder Corporation

4.   LIFE INSURANCE SOLICITATION: Rule 24

1   The purpose of the Solicitation Regulation is to provide **FULL DISCLOSURE** to the public by: (a) requiring Life Insurance Companies to provide Buyers/ Prospects with adequate information in order to select the most appropriate plan of Life insurance for their needs; (b) improving the Buyer's overall understanding of basic Life insurance policy types and features; and (c) providing pricing so Buyers can compare the relative costs of different Life insurance products.

2   The key to the Solicitation Regulation is **FULL DISCLOSURE**. This is a Consumer protection regulation.

3   FULL DISCLOSURE is provided to Buyers/Prospects/the Public through two documents, both designed/written by the National Association of Insurance Commissioners (NAIC):

A. The Buyer's Guide

4   The **Buyer's Guide** is a **generic brochure** that describes Life insurance **basics**; what is TERM, WHOLE LIFE, Cash Value, Surrender Value, dividends, death benefits, how much Life insurance the Applicant should purchase, and numerous indexes to determine and compare the relative values between policies from different insurance Companies

B. The Policy Summary

5   The **Policy Summary** summarizes the **specific policy** that the Buyer is considering purchasing. The Policy Summary includes a Statement Of Policy Costs and Benefits, the Policyowner's name and address, the name of the insurance Company, the type of Life insurance being purchased, the premium for the basic policy and for any riders attached to the policy, dividends (if any), policy loan interest rate, and the date.

6   The Buyer's Guide and the Policy Summary MUST be provided to all Applicants **PRIOR to accepting** the **Applicant's** initial **premium payment.**

7   The Solicitation Regulation does NOT apply to Group Life, Credit Life, Variable Life, or Annuities.

1 Rule 24 sets out what Producers and their Companies must do, and what they cannot do.

C. Some Important Points

2 The Solicitation Rule was promulgated/issued by the Insurance Commissioner to complement the **Unfair Competition Statute.** Thus Producers who violate this Rule would be liable to the penalties found in that statute.

3 Rule 24 defines *COST* of Life insurance as the **difference between what the Policyowner pays in premium, and what the policyowner gets back if they surrender the policy for its cash value.**

Premiums Paid – Cash Surrender Value = COST

4 Premium and benefit (which include surrender values) projections must be made for the **first five policy years**, or longer if needed to give an accurate picture of the policy.

5 In the case of a participating policy/contract, the Policy Summary must state that **Dividend projections** are based upon the Company's current level of dividend payments, and that Dividends are **NEVER** guaranteed.

D. Producer's Duties under Rule 24

1. As an **Insurance Producer**, you must inform the Applicant PRIOR to the beginning of your solicitation/sales presentation, that you are an **Insurance Producer.**

2. As an **Insurance Producer**, you must identify the name of the Company that you represent.

3. As an **Insurance Producer**, you may **NOT** use misleading terms to describe yourself, such as *Financial Planner, Financial Consultant, Investment Advisor,* or similar terms, because these terms often imply that you are involved in the transaction solely as a Financial Advisor, when the reality is that you are a Sales Agent/Producer working on commission.

4. You must advise the Applicant that **dividends are not guaranteed.**

© 2017 PATHFINDER Corporation

*NOTE: Although not part of Rule 24, it should be noted that all Life insurance policies must contain a **10 Day Free Look**. This is the Policyowner's absolute/unconditional right to return the policy to the Company for a full refund within 10 days of policy delivery.*

5. <u>LIFE INSURANCE REPLACEMENT: Rule 16.1</u>

Permanent Life insurance policies generally increase in value with age as the Cash Values grow. As a result, some Life insurance Companies have targeted existing cash value policies as vulnerable for replacement, and they have engaged in high-pressure sales tactics to convince Policyowners/ Consumers to replace their existing policies using their cash values. Often this is to the Consumer's detriment because the Policyowner:

1. Will pay another sales commission.

2. May no longer be insurable.

3. May spend part of their Cash Value to pay for the new policy.

4. Is at a higher attained age (may pay a higher Cost/Thousand for Life coverage).

5. Will need to endure another two year "Incontestable" period.

6. Will need to endure another two year "Suicide Clause" period.

As such, the State of Indiana has passed laws designed to protect existing Policyowners against indiscriminate replacement of their existing Life policies and Annuity contracts.

Replacement of existing Life policies is NOT illegal. Just highly regulated! There are situations where replacement is clearly warranted. But, such Replacement should only take place if it is in the Policyowner's best interest! Just follow the rules. Again, the emphasis is on FULL DISCLOSURE.

The Life Insurance Replacement Rules spell out the duties of Life insurance Companies and their Producers to ensure that the Public/ Policyowners are provided with adequate information to make an informed decision as to whether, or not, replacement is in their best interest.

SOME IMPORTANT POINTS

A. The Key Word: Disclosure

1   The entire purpose of Rule 16.1 is to provide the insuring Public with adequate information to make a good decision about keeping their existing Life policy, or to replace it with a new Life policy.

2   **Who initiates the idea** of Replacement, whether it is the Policyowner or the Producer, is irrelevant. If an existing Life policy is "replaced", and a new policy is purchased, Replacement has occurred, and the Replacement Rules must be followed.

3   Violations of Rule 16.1 are violations of the Unfair Competition Statute/Unfair Trade Practices Act. The Replacement Rule does not apply to **Group** or **Credit** insurance.

B. What Is *"Replacement"*?

4   **Replacement is defined as "Any transaction in which a new Life insurance policy is being purchased, and it is known, or should have been known (by the Producer), that as the result of this transaction, an existing Life policy will be:**

1. Lapsed, forfeited, surrendered, or terminated.

2. Converted (downgraded) to Reduced Paid Up, or Extended Term insurance, by use of the policy Non-forfeiture options (See the Pathfinder Text Chapter 6).

3. Amended to have a reduction in benefits, or in the length of the contract.

4. Reissued with a reduction in the policy's Cash Value.

5. Subjected to borrowing of more than **25%** of the Cash Value

In Indiana, the provisions of the Replacement Rule are triggered even if an insurance Company attempts to replace one of its own Life insurance policies.

© 2017 Pathfinder Corporation

C. Duties of the Producer

As a Producer, you MUST conduct a reasonable investigation as to whether Replacement will take place. This is reasonably simple, as there are numerous questions on the Application asking if Replacement will occur.

NOTE: The Producer's role is active, not passive.

D. If the Applicant IS NOT Replacing a Policy   NO

The Producer must ask if an Applicant intends to replace their existing/ current Life insurance policy. If the Applicant says that they **do not intend to replace** their existing policy, a statement to that effect must be signed by the Applicant and the Producer and submitted to the Producer's Company, stating that no Replacement is contemplated.

E. If the Applicant IS Replacing a Policy   YES

- The Producer must give to the Applicant a **signed** copy of the **Important Notice Regarding Replacement of Life Insurance**, as well as a copy of all sales proposals.

- The Producer must forward to their Company **signed** copies of all of the above documents, signed by both the Producer and the Applicant.

- The Replacing Company must notify the Existing Company within **3 working days** about the Replacement.

- The Existing Company, through its Producer, will then attempt to keep their existing policy alive/in force. This effort is known as **Conservation**.

- Replacement policies require a **20 Day Free Look**.   **20 Days**

IMPORTANT NOTE

<u>**TWISTING:**</u>   *Producers that Misrepresent the truth/lie during Replacement are guilty of* **"TWISTING"**.

© 2017 Pathfinder Corporation

6. MARKETING PRACTICES: LIFE INSURANCE ADVERTISING - Rule 13

1 Rule 13 is a laundry list of responsibilities, and prohibited practices, that Producers and Companies must follow in the marketing and sale of Life insurance, Annuities, and Health insurance contracts. DO NOT attempt to misrepresent, misinform, mislead, confuse, baffle, wow, or beguile the Public in "advertising". Tell the truth, the whole truth, and nothing but the truth!

2 Violations of Rule 13 are violations of the Unfair Competition & Practices Statute/ Unfair Trade Practices Act.

A. What is "Advertising"?

3 Insurance law defines "Advertising" as **"ANY communication directed to the consuming Public."**

4 The above definition would include broadcast, telecast, e-mail, web based, oral or written communications. TV, radio, billboards, print, newspapers, computer based, sky writing, Skype, Snoopy blimps, etc. is ALL advertising. And especially recognize that your **oral sales presentations are advertising!** So be very careful what you say! Or what you write on a napkin at a luncheon meeting with a Prospect!

5 The following is a partial list of Do's and Don'ts. Most of it is common sense.

B. Do's

1. All Applicants/Prospects must be informed up front by the Producer that the reason for the meeting is for the solicitation of Life/Health insurance.

2. All Producers must inform their Prospects who they are, and what insurance Company they represent.

3. All Life insurance policies must be clearly labeled as *LIFE INSURANCE*.

C. Don'ts: Prohibited Deceptive Practices

1. Life insurance policies, or Annuities, may not be called *Investment Plans, Founder's Plans, Profit Sharing Plans, Surplus Sharing Plans, etc.* which may infer that the Policyowner would receive something other than a Life insurance policy.

   Health insurance policies may not mislead the Public by using the following words: *All, Unlimited, Full, or Comprehensive;* or phrases such as *"This policy will pay your hospital bills;"* or *"This policy will replace your pay check,"* unless such statements accurately reflect the benefits found in the policy.

2. Policies may not be **"sold or serviced"** by the Company Investment Department which would infer that the Policyowner would receive special treatment/investment advice.

3. No solicitation for Life insurance may infer that the Prospect will receive **stock** in the insurance Company.

4. No solicitation may infer that the Prospect will receive **special treatment**, or a special advantage over other Policyowners.

5. No solicitation may infer that if the Prospect were to act as a **"Sphere of Influence"** for the Producer, that the Applicant would be given special benefits by the Company.

6. No Producer may infer to an Applicant/Policyowner that their premium payments are **"deposits"**. This infers that the Policyowner can withdraw the money any time as if it were a bank deposit.

7. And of course, dividends are **NEVER** guaranteed.

7. OTHER LAWS REGARDING SOLICITATION OF LIFE & HEALTH INSURANCE

A. Misrepresentations

1 The discussion of **Misrepresentation** in the Pathfinder text is limited to misrepresentations made by Applicants for insurance policies.

2 Indiana law also addresses **Misrepresentations** made by Insurance Companies and their Producers.

3 Indiana Law prohibits misrepresentations, not only as inducements to entice a Customer to purchase an insurance policy, but also those made to induce a Customer to allow an existing policy to lapse or otherwise be forfeited. (See the Replacement Regulation above.)

*Note: Violation of this statute is a **Crime** (Class A misdemeanor).*

B. Indiana Life & Heath Guaranty Association

4 Producers may not use the fact that their Company belongs to the Life and Health Guaranty Association as part of their sales presentation. If asked, however, you may explain the function of the Association. (See Section 1 of this Decoder for an explanation of the Association.)

C. Genetic Screening

5 Genetic screening and testing may **not** be used in making **underwriting** decisions in **health** insurance.

8. INDIANA LIFE POLICY PROVISIONS: KEY NUMBERS

Free Look:	10 days
Free Look - Replacement:	20 days
Backdating Apps:	6 months
Incontestable:	2 years
Reinstatement:	3 years
Lawsuits:	3 years
Maximum Loan Interest Rate:	8%
Cancellation for nonpayment of a Loan:	30 days

Death Benefits: Must be paid within **2 months** of Company's **receipt** of the Proof of Death.

Interest on Death Benefit: Begins to accrue **30 days** from the date the Company receives the Proof of Death.

The **interest rate** to be paid on the Death Benefit is the **same as** the policy loan interest rate.

9. LIVING BENEFIT OPTION #1: ACCELERATED DEATH BENEFITS - Rule 48

1   We think of Life insurance as only paying policy benefits when the Insured dies, which is reasonably true. But not always true. There are two "situations" in which Life policies DO pay "death" benefits to living Insured's. These are referred to as *Living Benefit Options*: **The Accelerated Death Benefit, and Viatical Settlements.** Both Options or Agreements require the Insured to be suffering a "near death" experience/life threatening **disease**, such as a terminal illness or a major organ failure. Death is imminent. In such a situation, the Insured may be able to obtain a substantial percentage of their policy's face value PRIOR TO THE INSURED'S ACTUAL DEATH! As a Living Benefit!

2   Rule 48 sets the ground rules for Accelerated Death Benefits (ADB) under Indiana law.

3   What happens if you own a Life insurance policy on your own life, are terminally ill, incurring huge medical bills to stay alive, and are running out of money? Well, if your policy has an **Accelerated Death Benefit**, either built in to your policy, or added as a Rider, you are in luck!

4   Under an Accelerated Death Benefit, your insurance Company will pay you as the Insured Policyowner a percentage of the policy FACE AMOUNT/ DEATH BENEFIT if you qualify for the ADB. The Company will then pay the **remaining balance** of the death benefit to your designated Beneficiary upon your actual death.

5   Accelerated Death Benefit provisions and riders are regulated under Indiana law as life **insurance**, and not health insurance, e.g., they are rated on the basis of **mortality**, and not morbidity.

6   The cost of ADB provisions, or riders, must be fully disclosed to the Applicant.

A. ADB Qualifying Events

The Insured is one or more of the following:

1. **Terminally ill**, with a life span estimated to be 24 months or less.

2. A medical condition which allows the Insured to survive only with **extraordinary medical intervention**, e.g. an organ transplant or continuous artificial life support: Example; *Need a kidney.*

3. Any condition which requires the Insured to be **permanently institutionalized.** *One way trip to a nursing home.*

4. Any medical condition which, absent extensive treatment, **drastically limits the Insured's life span**, such as heart disease, cancer, or renal failure = *Body shutting down.*

5. And, of course, the ultimate catch-all: Any other condition approved by the Commissioner: *"Because I said so."*

*NOTE: Should the Policyowner have **assigned** the policy, named a Beneficiary on an Irrevocable basis, or pledged the policy benefits, permission of the "Assignee" must be obtained prior to triggering the Accelerated Death Benefits. Prior permission from a Revocable Beneficiary, however, is NOT necessary.*

B. Benefit Payment as a Lump Sum

The contract **must allow** for the payment of the Accelerated Death Benefit to the Policyowner/Insured as a **lump sum**. There may be no restrictions on how the money may be spent by the Policyowner/Insured.

C. Premium Requirements after an ADB Payment

Policies may offer either a specific Accelerated Death Benefit **Waiver of Premium**, or a standard Waiver of Premium. However, should the policy contain neither, the Company shall fully explain the premium requirements necessary to keep the policy in force.

For those policies that have cash value, the reductions of such cash values can be no greater than the **pro rata** portion of the ADB payment. For example, if 60% of the policy death benefit is paid out to the Insured as a ADB, then the policy's cash value cannot be reduced by more than 60%.

D. Reduced Death Benefit Paid to Beneficiary

The payment of an Accelerated Death Benefit to the Policyowner/Insured is a lien on any remaining death benefit. Therefore, the Beneficiary will receive only the remainder of the unpaid death benefit. For example, if the Insured received 60% of a $100,000 Face Amount Life policy, or $60,000, and then died, the Named Beneficiary would receive the remaining $40,000.

10. LIVING BENEFIT AGREEMENT #2: VIATICAL SETTLEMENTS

1
If you are dying (terminally ill/face a life threatening disease), and IF your Life insurance policy has an Accelerated Death Benefit, you would certainly use it if you needed the money. But what if your Life policy does NOT have an Accelerated Death Benefit? Then a **Viatical Settlement** is an option/alternative. (*Viatical* is Latin for "In danger of death.")

2
Under a Viatical Settlement contract, you as the Policyowner/Insured **SELL** your policy (at a discount) to an Investor, called a Viatical, or Viatical Settlement Provider. The Viatical purchases your policy for less than its Face Value as an investment, in an attempt to make a profit. This is a **Third Party transaction** because the agreement is NOT between you and your insurance Company. A Viatical contract is with an entirely new and different entity = a Third Party.

3
The Viatical Settlement Company purchases your Life insurance contract from you for less than its Face Value. How much you will receive is dependent on your life expectancy and the discount rate used.

4
You make an **Absolute Assignment** of your policy to the Viatical Settlement Company, which makes the Viatical the new Policyowner. Then the Viatical names itself as the new **Beneficiary**. You are still the Insured.

© 2017 Pathfinder Corporation

A. Key Definitions

1. Viatical Settlement Company = The Third Party Buyer/Investor who purchases the Life policy and becomes the new Policyowner and Beneficiary.

2. Viatical Producer = An Agent that represents a Viatical Settlement Company. Seeks the "Living Dead" to purchase their Life policies.

3. Viatical Broker = An Agent that represents the dying Insured/Policyowner. Attempts to arrange a Viatical Settlement for their Client.

4. Viator = The Insured/Policyowner who is dying, and seeking to sell their policy for cash.

Please keep in mind:

I. ACCELERATED DEATH BENEFITS • **Two party contracts** • **Funds to Insured Policyowner comes from insurance Company**
II. VIATICAL SETTLEMENTS • **Third party contracts** • **Funds to Insured Policyowner comes from Third Party Investor (Viatical)**

B. What Does the Viatical Statute Do?

The statute regulates not only the Viatical Settlement contracts, but also Viatical Settlement Companies, Viatical Producers, Viatical Brokers, and the Viators/Insured's.

C. Some Important Points

1. Viatical Settlements can be referred to as simply *Viaticals*, or **Living Benefit Agreements**.

2. All Viatical Settlement Companies/Providers, and their Producers, must be **licensed** to market Viatical Settlement Contracts by the Indiana Department of the Insurance.

3. Viatical Producers and Brokers must also be licensed as Life Insurance Producers.

4. Viatical Settlement Providers must file annual reports to the IDOI, and are subject to **examination**.

5. The statute contains several reasons for suspension of a Provider's license, such as: **"a pattern of unreasonable payment."**

D. Full Disclosure of the Details

6. Viatical Settlement Providers, through their Viatical Producers, must follow strict rules of disclosure during the settlement process, which include:

   - Possible alternatives, such as borrowing the cash value.

   - Tax consequences.

   - The possible interruption of certain benefits as a result of the Viatical transaction, such as losing Medicaid benefits.

   - The requirement for the **longer of**: a **30 Day Free Look** from date of the execution of the contract, or **15 Days** from the receipt of the first check.

7. The "Insured" must also execute a document making full disclosure of their medical condition, as well as their understanding of the transaction and its consequences.

8. The 'Insured's" doctor must also attest to the Insured/Policyowner's competency to enter into the Viatical contract.

11. GROUP LIFE

A. Eligible Groups

Please see the Pathfinder L&H text, Chapter 16, regarding Eligible Groups for Group Life Insurance. They include:

- **Single Employers**
- **Labor Unions**
- **Associations**
- **Creditors**
- **Credit Unions**

B. Group Conversion Rights To Individual Policy

1 A *Conversion Right* is a right granted to a Group Life member to have issued to them, upon leaving the Group, an individual Life policy. No Evidence of Insurability is required. (They could be uninsurable and still get the Life insurance policy).

2 If a Group Life policy issued in Indiana contains a **Conversion Right**, normally the departing member has 31 days from the date they terminated their employment to complete the conversion (**Conversion Period**). But what happens if the Employer does NOT inform the departing employee of their Conversion Rights?

3 In Indiana, a departing Employee is given an ADDITIONAL 15 DAYS from the date of Employer notification in order to make the conversion.

4 However, this extended Conversion Period cannot exceed a total of 60 days from employment termination.

CONVERSION SUMMARY - INDIANA

Normal Conversion Period	31 Days
Extension	15 Days
Maximum Conversion Period	60 Days

12. LIFE PRODUCER MANDATORY ANNUITY TRAINING

Indiana state law requires that **ALL** Resident and Nonresident **Life Insurance Producers** must attend a one time **four hour Annuities** continuing education training course BEFORE selling, soliciting, or negotiating Life Insurance and/or Annuity Contracts. This requirement is on a one-time basis.

© 2017 Pathfinder Corporation

INDIANA HEALTH LAWS, RULES & REGULATIONS

8 Questions

1. <u>HEALTH INSURANCE ADVERTISING: Rule 18</u>

1 Rule 18 is the Health version of Rule 13 *Life Insurance Advertising*. Please review Rule 13 in the Life Regulations section which is essentially the same as Rule 18.

2 One minor difference is that Rule 18 places more emphasis on requiring Health Insurance Companies to give equal emphasis to policy **limitations and exclusions** as are given to policy benefits. The Company **must state the bad, as well as the good.**

And Remember: A Producer's oral sales presentation is *advertising*.

3 Again, Rule 18 warns against the use of words such as: "All, Full, Comprehensive, Unlimited", and phrases such as "This policy will pay your hospital bills," or "This policy will replace your paycheck," unless such statements accurately reflect the benefits found in the policy.

4 Also, Insurance Companies or their Agents/Producers **cannot** imply that they are connected with any government agencies, such as the Social Security Administration, Medicare or Medicaid, or the IDOI.

2. FINE TUNING THE UNIFORM INDIVIDUAL & GROUP HEALTH POLICY PROVISIONS LAWS

Please review the Uniform Individual Health Policy Provisions Laws found in Chapter 15 of the Pathfinder L&H text, and Group Health Standard Policy Provisions found in Chapter 17. The Group Provisions are almost identical to the Individual Provisions, with a few minor exceptions as noted below.

Indiana Individual Provisions Requirements

A. The maximum **Pre-existing Conditions Exclusion is 12 months.**

B. The most restrictive definition of a **Pre-existing Condition** is one "For which a person reasonably would have sought medical treatment."

C. The maximum **Incontestable Period** is **2 years.**

D. Should an Insured die during the term of a Health Policy, the Company **must refund any unearned premium.**

E. Under the NAIC Model Health Provisions, the **Relation to Earnings Provision** is optional, but it is **mandatory** under Indiana Law. Therefore, Indiana Disability Income Policies **MUST** contain a **Relation to Earnings Provision.** This provision keeps an individual from profiting from a disability by over-insuring themselves.

The clause stipulates that:

1. In the event that an Insured's actual earnings have averaged **less than** the benefits promised in the policy for the **2 years** prior to the claim, the amount of the benefits paid shall be reduced on a **pro rata** basis. In other words, if an Insured has earned **less income** in the past two years than the benefit level of their Disability Income policy, the policy benefits paid will be reduced if the Insured suffers a loss.

2. But, in no case will benefits drop below **$200 per month.**

3. If an Insured's Disability Income benefits have been reduced because their income has decreased, and now they are over-insured, the Insured shall be entitled to a **pro rata refund of premium** for up to a 2 year period.

F. The ***Terminating Age/Limiting Age*** for dependent children covered by a medical expense policy is **age 26.**

Group Provisions

A. ***Time of Payment of Claims Provision:*** Whereas Individual medical expense claims must be paid ***immediately***, Group medical expense claims must be paid **within 60 days.**

3. MAMMOGRAPHY: BREAST CANCER SCREENING- A REQUIRED COVERAGE

Breast Cancer Screening Mammography (BCSM) coverage **MUST** be offered by every Medical Expense policy delivered in Indiana. The woman and her doctor, *not* the insurance Company, control the testing and procedures.

Specifically, BCSM minimum benefits are:

1. Every woman between the **ages of 35 and 40 will be** entitled to one **base line** BCSM.

2. Every woman over **age 40 will** be entitled to **one per year.**

3. Every woman classified as a ***Woman at Risk***, regardless of age (see below) will be entitled to **one per year.**

© 2017 Pathfinder Corporation

4. Any other mammograms that the doctor considers necessary for proper evaluation.

Young Healthy Women: *between ages 35 and 40*	One Base Line
Women over age 40:	One per year
Women *at Risk*:	One per year

A ***Woman at Risk*** is defined as a woman:

- Who has a personal history of breast cancer.

- Who has a personal history of breast disease that was proven benign.

- Whose mother, sister or daughter has had breast cancer.

- Who is over age 30, and has not given birth.

4.   RIGHTS OF DEPENDENT CHILDREN

1   In Indiana, like most States, **dependent children**, including **adopted children**, are granted substantial rights under both Individual and Group health medical expense policies. Please review these rights as found at the conclusion of Chapter 12 in the Pathfinder Life & Health textbook.

2   A summary of dependent children's rights is as follows.

3   In either Individual or Group medical expense plans, if the policy extends benefits to dependent children, then:

A. Coverage for newborns begins at the **moment of birth**.

B. Coverage for adopted children begins at *Date of Placement.*

C. No Proof of Insurability is required. The kids are automatically covered!

D. Maternity Benefit coverage (have it, or don't have it) does NOT affect the coverage for newborns or adopted children.

E. The Policyowner must notify the insurance Company of the child **within 31 days.**

F. If **additional premium** is due for the child, the premium must be paid to the Company **within 31 days** to have coverage for the child go beyond the 31st day.

G. The **limiting age** for dependent coverage is **age 26**. Then your "kids" are on their own!

H. **Incapacitated & Handicapped Dependents** - However, coverage can NOT be terminated on a dependent child over age 26 who is, and continues to be, both of the following:

1. Incapable of self-sustaining employment because of physical handicap or mental retardation, and

2. Chiefly dependent upon the Policyowner for support and maintenance.

3. Proof of such incapacity must be furnished to the Company within 31 days of reaching age 26.

4. During the next two years, the Company may require proof of continued incapacity and dependence at reasonable intervals.

5. After the two year period, the Company may require subsequent proof no more frequently than once each year.

5. INDIANA COMPREHENSIVE HEALTH INSURANCE ASSOCIATION (ICHIA)

A. The Problem

1   What happens if an Indiana Resident becomes **uninsurable**, or cannot purchase Health insurance at a reasonable price?

2   Hoosiers are fortunate because the State of Indiana provides an opportunity for Health coverage through the **Indiana Comprehensive Health insurance Association (ICHIA) Plan.**

B. The Solution

3   **ICHIA is a High Risk Pool.** The Pool creates a way for Hoosiers, who are otherwise uninsurable, or cannot find medical expense coverage at reasonable rates, the opportunity to buy Health insurance coverage at somewhat more reasonable rates.

C. What Does The Statute Do?

4   The statute creates the Pool/Association (ICHIA), and requires that ALL Admitted Health Insurance Companies must be a member of the Association. The statute also sets the maximum premium rates, and mandates the benefits, deductible and co-insurance limits.

D. How does ICHIA work?

5   All members of the pool split the risk. However, the policies are issued by an individual insurance company who acts as the *Servicing Insurer.*

1. **Eligibility:** Any Indiana resident who cannot buy health insurance through normal channels at premiums lower than the ICHIA rates.

2. **Benefits:** The coverage is essentially Major Medical.

3. **Premium:** No more the **150%** of the average **standard** premium charged by the state's **5 largest** Health insurers.

4. **Deductibles:** The maximum deductible is **$500 per person** per year.

5. **Coinsurance:** The maximum coinsurance percentage is **20%**.

6. **Maximum Out-Of-Pocket Expenses:** The maximum out-of-pocket expense is **$1500 per individual,** and **$2500 per family per year**.

7. **Exclusions:** Expenses covered by Medicare, Medicaid, Workers Compensation, or any no-fault auto benefit (Med Pay) are not covered by ICHIA. In addition, **Custodial or Residential Care LTC and elective cosmetic surgeries** are excluded.

8. **Preexisting Conditions:** The maximum Preexisting Conditions period is **3 months.** However, if the insured applies for ICHIA coverage within 6 months of losing coverage under another Medical Expense plan, then there will be no Exclusion for Preexisting Conditions.

6. <u>SPECIAL TREATMENT FOR INDIANA SMALL GROUP HEALTH – SMALL EMPLOYER GROUPS</u>

A. Why?

Group health insurance operates under one simple rule, i.e., the bigger the Group, the better the deal. In recent history smaller employers have had difficulty buying health insurance at reasonable rates. This statute is a legislative attempt to level the playing field.

B. What Does the Statute Do?

The Statute sets standards for carriers/insurers that enter the **Small Group Health** market, as well as regulating the policies that they sell.

C. Some Important Points

A **Small Employer Group** under Indiana Law is defined as one having anywhere from **2 to 50** employees.

1   A Group health plan under this statute includes not only traditional insurance plans, but also hospital and medical service plans, HMOs and employer-funded (ERISA) health plans.

D. Keys Elements of the Small Group Statute

1. **No "Cherry Picking"** – Insurers which issue coverage to members of a Small Employer Group **must accept all eligible employees** and their dependents. The law does not allow carriers to limit coverage to part of a group, or specific individuals within a group.

2. **Late Enrollees** –   A Late Enrollee is defined as an eligible employee or dependent who failed to request coverage **when they first became eligible** to enroll in the health plan.

3. **Not a "Late Enrollee"** – An individual who was covered under another medical expense plan, such as under COBRA from a former employer, when they first became eligible for benefits under their Small Group Employer plan, and accordingly refused the coverage at their new place of employment during the COBRA period, is NOT a "Late Enrollee".

4. **Preexisting Conditions** – Preexisting Conditions can be excluded for up to **9 months** from the effective date of coverage. However, for a Late Enrollee, benefits can be excluded for up to **15 months.** The reason for a longer exclusion period is simple... **Adverse Selection.** Employees may delay enrolling in the plan until they become ill. Then they would join, and expect instant coverage.

Preexisting Conditions Exclusion:

*Benefits can be excluded for up to 9 **months**. Benefits can be excluded for Late Enrollees for up to 15 **months**.*

---

5. **Portability – HIPAA LITE:** If a new Employee was previously covered by a Group medical expense health plan:

   A. Which provided approximately the same coverage as the new Employer's plan, and…

   B. The Employee was covered within **30 days** from the time that they became eligible for the new Employer's health insurance plan, then…

   C. There will be **NO exclusions in coverage for Preexisting Conditions.**

6. **Conversion Privileges –** Employees covered by Small Employer Group plans, who have been covered continuously for more than **90 days,** shall have the **right to convert** their coverage to individual policies, if they lose Group coverage because of:

   A. Termination of employment.

   B. Reduction of hours.

   C. Dissolution of their marriage.

   D. Attaining an age specified in the Group policy.

   E. Conversion must be requested within 30 days.

7. **Maximum Premium –** The premium for the converted individual policy shall be limited to **150%** of the Group rate.

8. **Benefit Levels –** If the benefits in the new policy are not greater than those under the Group plan, the Insurer shall credit the Employee with any waiting periods, deductibles, or coinsurance they paid or were charged under the Group plan.

NOTE: All converted policies shall also be subject to all of the special requirements for Small Employer Group policies.

Numbers recap	
Small Groups	2-50 Employees
Preexisting Conditions exclusion	9 months
Preexisting Conditions exclusion for Late Enrollees	15 months
Number of days to convert	30 days
Maximum premium after conversion	150%

7. CHILDREN'S HEALTH INSURANCE PROGRAM: CHIP

1   The Indiana Children's Health Insurance Program **(CHIP)** is designed to provide coverage for children if their family's income is too high to qualify for Medicaid benefits, and they cannot afford health insurance elsewhere.

In order to qualify for coverage under CHIP, a child must

1. Be less than age 19.

2. Be from a family with an income more than 150%, but less than 200%, of the Federal Poverty level.

3. Be a Resident of Indiana.

4. Meet the eligibility requirements of Title XIX Medicaid of the Social Security Act.

The child's family must agree to pay all required Co-payments.

2   Children who are declared eligible for CHIP will receive benefits for a minimum of 12 consecutive months (unless they turn age 19 during that period). The coverage is similar to Major Medical insurance.

8. GROUP COORDINATION OF BENEFITS: Rule 38.1

A. The Problem

1   Suppose Joe Insured works for ABC Corporation where he and all of his dependents are covered by the ABC Group Major Medical insurance plan. His Spouse, Jolene Insured, works for XYZ Corporation where she and all of her dependents (including Joe) are covered by the XYZ Group Major Medical plan. Both Joe and Jolene are double covered. Then assume that Joe has a covered loss. Will he be able to collect twice for his loss, and profit from the loss? For the answer, see **Section D**.

B. The Solution: Coordination of Benefits Clause

2   The primary purpose for the Group Coordination of Benefits provision in Group Major Medical policies is to ensure that an insured who is double covered **does benefit** from the double coverage, but **does NOT make a profit** from the double coverage.

1. The **purpose** of the Group Coordination of Benefits/Rule 38.1 is to:

   a. Allow, but not require, medical expense plans to include a **Coordination of Benefits** provision.

   b. Establish the priority of claim payments.

   c. Provide a channel for claim information, to ensure more timely payments.

   d. Reduce the opportunity for the Insured to profit from a loss.

   e. Reduce claim payment delays.

   f. Establish consistency in policy provisions.

1 The **Coordination of Benefits Rule** applies only to Group Medical Expense coverages, whether paying on a reimbursement or service basis, but not policies such as Auto medical payments, hospital indemnification, Medicare, etc. For a more complete discussion as to the purpose of the Rule, please see Chapter 17 of the Pathfinder L&H text, which discusses the NAIC Model Coordination of Benefits Provision. Rule 38.1 incorporates this Provision by reference.

The following are the additional regulations found in Indiana Rule 38.1.

C. Primary and Secondary

2 The **Primary Coverage** is the policy that covers the sick/injured individual who is making the claim. Primary plans **may in no way reduce the benefits** as the result of the existence of a Secondary Plan.

3 A **Secondary Coverage** is any plan which is not Primary. Example: a husband's Primary plan would be the one offered to him by his Employer. His coverage as a dependent under his wife's plan would be Secondary.

D. An Example

4 If you remember from Section A, Joe Insured is an employee of ABC Corporation and is covered by ABC's Group Major Medical plan. The ABC plan covers his spouse and his dependents as well. Jolene Insured works for XYZ Corporation where she is covered by the XYZ Group Major Medical plan. The XYZ plan also covers spouses and their dependents. So both Joe and Jolene Insured are **double covered**. Also suppose that each plan has a $500 deductible, and an 80/20% Coinsurance clause.

If Joe Insured suffered a $10,500 covered loss, the claim would be paid as follows:

Loss =	$10,500	
Minus the Deductible	- 500	*normally Joe would pay this*
Balance	$10,000	
ABC Insurance Co pays 80% =	- 8,000	
Remainder =	$ 2,000	*normally Joe would pay this*

So, if there was no double coverage, Joe would pay the $500 Deductible, plus the $2,000 Coinsurance amount, for a total of $2,500. But, because there IS double coverage, the Secondary Insurer, XYZ, will pay what the Primary Insurer, ABC, won't pay, which is the $2,500. So Joe will pay nothing! But please note, while Joe DID benefit by being double covered, HE DID NOT MAKE A PROFIT, which would violate the Rule of Indemnification.

E. Children

The plan of the parent **whose birthday comes first in the year** would be the Primary plan for the children. Should the parents have the same birth date, the plan which has been in effect the longest shall be Primary. In the case of divorce or separation, the plan of that parent which is the subject of the support order shall be Primary.

9. LONG TERM CARE (LTC) & MEDICARE SUPPLEMENT POLICIES (MSP)

Please review LTC and MSP policies in Chapter 14 in the Pathfinder L&H text. Indiana Regulations are essentially the same as those in the text, as they comply with the NAIC Model LTC and MSP legislation.

A. Key LTC/MSP Characteristics & Policy Provisions

1. LTC **minimum benefit/ coverage length = 12 months**

2. Eligibility requirements

3. Definition of terms

4. Preexisting Conditions/Probationary Periods = no more than **6 months**

5. Must be Guaranteed Renewable or Noncancellable

6. **Mandatory** inflation protection for LTCP (optional for LTC policies)

7. Graphic comparison of inflation protected benefit levels

8. Group Conversion Rights

9. Non-Duplication of other health care coverages

10. **Notice Regarding Replacement of Health Insurance**

© 2017 Pathfinder Corporation

11. **Suitability Statement =** Producer's written statement saying that they have reviewed the Applicant's health care coverages, and the Producer's recommendations are in the Applicant's best interest.

12. **30 Day Free Look**

13. LTC Continuing Educational requirements (see below).

14. Disclosure and Performance Standards, such as the maximum Preexisting Conditions period **is 6 months**.

15. **Shopper's Guide** and **Outline of Coverage** requirements.

16. Policy Summary requirement

17. Loss Ratio requirement

18. Policy Exclusions

19. Reasons for policy Cancellation/Nonrenewal

20. Producer's commission structure

21. Prohibition against **Twisting** (lying during the replacement of insurance) and **high pressure sales tactics.**

B. LTC and MSP Marketing Requirements/Producer's Duties

Again, please review the LTC and MSP marketing requirements discussed near the end of Chapter 13 of the Pathfinder L&H text. They include the following:

1. Producers must ask LTC/MSP Prospects if they have any existing LTC or MSP policies. THERE CAN BE NO DUPLICATION OF COVERAGES!

2. Are they covered by Medicaid?

3. Have they recently cancelled any LTC/MSP policies?

4. Are they going to cancel any health coverages as the result of purchasing new coverage?

5. Producers MUST do a thorough review of all existing coverages to make certain that any recommendations are **SUITABLE**, and in the best interests of the Client/Applicant.

6. All policy comparisons must be fair and accurate.

7. Excessive amounts of insurance must NOT be recommended.

8. Full explanations of policy benefits and Exclusions must be given.

9. If Replacement is involved, provide a copy of the **Important Notice Regarding the Replacement of Health Insurance.**

C. But There is Something Even Better than LTC!

As good as the basic LTC policy is, a person with an LTC policy must still consume virtually their entire net worth before they are eligible for Medicaid (often referred to the **Medicaid "Spend Down"**). The LTC policy would pay benefits up to its policy limits, and then the Insured would have to pay the nursing home costs until they ran out of money. Only then, would the person be eligible for Medicaid benefits. But, Indiana has a better way, and it is called The **LTC Partnership Program**! Read on!

10. THE INDIANA LTCP: THE PARTNERSHIP PROGRAM = ASSET PROTECTION PROGRAM

At the present time, the only **government** program that will pay for a long-term care (LTC) nursing home stay is **Medicaid.**

But to qualify for Medicaid, you must be **poor/broke**. Quite often Senior Citizens are forced to go through the Medicaid **spend down** in order to qualify for Medicaid. Seniors essentially must divest themselves of almost all their assets that they have spent a lifetime acquiring, which is most unfortunate. A better answer is the Indiana Long Term Care Partnership Program (LTCP).

The Partnership program gives individuals who purchase **qualified** LTC policies the opportunity to **shelter assets from the Medicaid spend down.** A "**qualified**" plan is an LTC policy approved by the State of Indiana that contains certain characteristics as explained on the next page.

A. How does the LTCP Asset Protection Plan work?

1. Assume for a minute that in order to be eligible for Medicaid, an individual would have to have less than $3,000 in assets. This means that in order to have Medicaid pay for their nursing home stay, they could possess no more than $3,000 in assets.

2. The LTCP program shelters a dollar's worth of assets for every dollar's worth of Long Term Care insurance that the Policyowner purchases.

3. For example, assume that an Individual purchases a qualified LTCP policy with a benefit level of $100,000. Should the person need nursing home care, their LTC policy would pay for the first $100,000 in LTC expenses. At that time, the individual would qualify for Medicaid, even though their net worth is $103,000. They have **protected their assets**/sheltered a sum equal to the policy benefit limits of their LTC policy, and have avoided the Medicaid *spend down* by $100,000. The individual can now use the $100,000 to fund a better quality of life during their golden years, or leave the hard earned money to their family.

B. LTCP Marketing Requirements

1. Full disclosure must be made to Prospects regarding the LTCP program.

2. LTC policies which qualify for the LTCP program must contain a statement to this effect as part of the **Outline of Coverage.**

3. All Applicants must be informed of the IDOI "hotline" for the FREE Senior Health Insurance Information Program.

4. A complete explanation of the **Asset Protection Program** must be given.

5. LTCP policies must contain **Mandatory Inflation Protection** which is the automatic increase in the nursing home daily rate provided by the policy to match inflation. The premiums can be adjusted accordingly.

6. **30 Day Free Look**

7. LTCP benefits must be expressed in **Dollars, not Days.**

8. Minimum Producer training requirements as stated on the next page.

© 2017 Pathfinder Corporation

C. Producer Education Requirements

1   All Producers selling LTC must complete **8 hours** of post-licensing LTC Continuing Education. They must also devote a portion of their required future Continuing Education (CE) hours to LTC courses (currently 5 hours every two years).

2   Rule 2 requires that licensed Producers wishing to market the LTCP/Asset Protection program must take an **additional seven (7) hour course** on the LTCP program, for a total of **15 hours** post-licensing education.

LTC Only	**8 Hours of education**
LTC & LTCP	**15 Hours of education**

11. <u>SUMMARY OF FREE LOOKS</u>

By now, you are Free Looked to death! So, here is a summary!

Ordinary Life or Health Policies	10 Days
Replacing Life or Health policies	20 Days
Senior Citizen Policies LTC & MSP & Viatical Settlements	30 Days

© 2017 Pathfinder Corporation

INDIANA GENERAL INSURANCE REGULATIONS QUIZ

1.   All of the following are requirements that you must meet in order to obtain an Indiana insurance Producer's license EXCEPT

   (A)   Make application with the Department of Insurance.
   (B)   Pass the licensing examination given by the Commissioner or persons selected by the Commissioner.
   (C)   Obtain the sponsorship of an admitted insurance company.
   (D)   Complete an approved prelicensing course.

2.   You are employed by an Indiana insurance agency to talk to prospective clients about your company's insurance policies. When a prospect wishes to purchase insurance, a licensed Producer in the office completes the application for you and signs the forms. You do not sign anything because you are unlicensed. You are acting as a(an)

   (A)   Consultant.
   (B)   Surplus Lines Producer.
   (C)   Limited Lines Producer.
   (D)   Unlicensed Producer.

3.   All of the following may obtain a limited insurance Producer's license EXCEPT

   (A)   A person selling baggage insurance in a transportation terminal.
   (B)   A person selling travel accident insurance in a transportation terminal.
   (C)   A person selling title insurance to the purchaser of real estate.
   (D)   A person selling limited health policies (such as cancer insurance) to church members.

4.   Though the Commissioner may issue a limited insurance Producer's license without requiring an examination, he currently administers an exam to which of the following limited insurance Producers?

   (A)   Those selling flight policies in transportation terminals.
   (B)   Funeral Directors selling pre-need burial plans.
   (C)   Those selling title insurance in connection with real estate transactions.
   (D)   Those selling baggage insurance in transportation terminals.

5. All of the following are required of an individual seeking an Indiana Non Resident Producers License EXCEPT

(A) Be licensed as a resident Producer in their home state.
(B) The Producer's home state has reciprocity with Indiana.
(C) The proper application has been submitted.
(D) The individual pass the State Law portion of the Indiana Licensing Exam.

6. If the Commissioner finds you guilty of violating Producer Licensing Law, all of the following may occur EXCEPT

(A) You may have your license revoked or suspended.
(B) You may be jailed for up to 365 days.
(C) You may be fined up to $10,000.
(D) A hearing will be held, should you request it.

7. Bill Black and Dave Decker have formed a partnership known as the Black and Decker Insurance Agency. If Bill becomes permanently and totally disabled, the Commissioner could grant a temporary license to all of the following EXCEPT

(A) Bill's wife.
(B) Bill's guardian.
(C) one of Bill's employees.
(D) the partnership itself.

8. As set forth in Indiana law, all of the following are considered to be unfair insurance trade practices EXCEPT

(A) Making an untrue, deceptive or misleading statement about a competitor.
(B) Making a maliciously critical statement about the financial condition of an insurance company.
(C) Lowering the premiums paid by an employer for group insurance based upon loss experiences.
(D) Restraining trade.

9. Al and Betty Franken wish to obtain a mortgage from Clamdigger's National Bank. The bank wants them to insure the property that is to be mortgaged. Which is true concerning the bank's request?

   (A) The bank can legally require that the property be insured, and that the insurance must be purchased from the bank.
   (B) The bank can legally require that the property be insured, but it cannot require that the insurance be purchased from the bank.
   (C) The bank cannot legally require that the property be insured nor that any insurance which is purchased be purchased from the bank.
   (D) The bank cannot legally require that the property be insured, but it can require that any insurance purchased on the property be purchased from the bank.

10. If the Commissioner has reason to believe that you have violated the Unfair Competition Law, several events may occur. These include all of the following EXCEPT

   (A) The Commissioner may conduct a hearing after giving you at least 5 days written notification.
   (B) Based upon his findings, at a hearing the Commissioner can issue a cease-and-desist order.
   (C) You may request a judicial review of the Commissioner's order.
   (D) You are subject to a fine of not more than $1,000 for each violation, not to exceed $5,000 in any 6-month period.

11. If the Commissioner issues a cease-and-desist order and you continue the same activities, you can be fined up to which of the following amounts per violation of that order?

   (A) $ 1,000
   (B) $ 5,000
   (C) $25,000
   (D) $50,000

12. Under the Unfair Competition Statute

   (A) Premiums may not be based upon the age or gender of an applicant.
   (B) Participating policies must guarantee dividends.
   (C) Rebates may be paid to consumers, if it is in "the public interest."
   (D) Financial institutions may require insurance on the lives of debtors.

13. Jack is licensed as a Life Producer and Jill is licensed as a Property and Casualty Producer. Jack sends one of his Life insurance clients to Jill to buy automobile insurance. Jill makes the sale and sends a portion of her commission to Jack who accepts it. Which is true concerning these events?

   (A) This transaction would be illegal because you cannot share the commissions with a Producer who does not have the same Line of Authority.
   (B) Jack and Jill are guilty of Rebating.
   (C) Jack and Jill are allowed to share the commission in this manner.
   (D) Jack and Jill are guilty of violating the Controlled Business Regulations.

14. All of the following are true regarding controlled business EXCEPT

   (A) Controlled business includes insurance written on your parents.
   (B) Controlled business includes insurance written on yourself.
   (C) The limit for controlled business is 25% of the premium that you write in a year.
   (D) The limit for controlled business is 25% of your commission income in a twelve month period.

15. A Producer may collect both a consulting fee and a commission in the same transaction if

   (A) The Producer is also licensed as a consultant.
   (B) The Producer is also licensed as a surplus lines Producer.
   (C) The Producer is also a licensed broker.
   (D) The Producer makes full disclosure in writing about the compensation arrangements prior to the time that the transaction occurs.

16. A full lines Producer renewing a two year license must have

   (A) 10 Hours of Continuing education.
   (B) 15 Hours of Continuing education.
   (C) 24 Hours of Continuing education.
   (D) 30 Hours of Continuing education.

17. The Commissioner must be notified in all of the following circumstances EXCEPT:

   (A) A Producer changes their business address.
   (B) A Producer changes their residential address.
   (C) A Producer is discharged for cause by an insurance company.
   (D) A Producer changes their telephone number.

INDIANA GENERAL INSURANCE REGULATIONS QUIZ

18. All of the following are true EXCEPT

   (A) The Commissioner may examine any company doing business in Indiana at any time.
   (B) The Commissioner must examine all companies doing business in Indiana at least every five years.
   (C) The Commissioner may waive the examination for a domestic company, under certain circumstances.
   (D) The Commissioner may waive the examination for a foreign or alien company under certain circumstances.

19. All of the following are qualifications of a resident Producer EXCEPT

   (A) They must be an Indiana resident.
   (B) They must be at least 21 years of age.
   (C) They must have passed an examination.
   (D) They must have completed an approved prelicensing course.

END

QUIZ ANSWERS & EXPLANATIONS ON NEXT PAGE

© 2017 Pathfinder Corporation

INDIANA GENERAL INSURANCE REGULATIONS
QUIZ ANSWER KEY

1.   C.   An application, a successful test, and prelicensing education are necessary for a license; appointment by a company is not.

2.   D.   Anyone who solicits, negotiates or sells is acting as a Producer. To act legally these persons must be licensed.

3.   D.   The others are dealing with the general public, not a closed group.

4.   B.   Funeral Directors, and their employees who are also licensed funeral directors may obtain a limited license to sell pre-need insurance, after completing the necessary prelicensing course and passing the examination.

5.   D.   No examination is required for a non-resident license, if the Producer is in good standing in her home state, she has made application, and the home state has reciprocity with Indiana.

6.   B.   The Commissioner cannot jail anyone; only a Judge has that power.

7.   D.   A temporary license may only be issued to a human being.

8.   C.   This is an acceptable and common practice in group insurance known as experience rating.

9.   B.   The Unfair Competition law allows lenders to demand insurance, the lender can also offer the insurance. The lender cannot however make the purchase of insurance from them a requirement for the loan.

10.   D.   The limits for fines are $25K per violation for unknowing violations and $50K per violation for knowing violations of the law.

11.   C.   This is in addition to any fine imposed for the violation itself.

12.   D.   Remember that they can require the insurance, just not that the insurance be purchased from them.

13.   C.   Bulletin 177 states that Producers may share commissions, even though they do not have the same Lines of Author, as long as the Non-Qualified Producer does not participate in the sale.

14.   C.   Controlled business is based on commission income earned in a rolling twelve-month period. Controlled business is any insurance written on your interests, those of your employer, employees, or immediate family.

© 2017 Pathfinder Corporation

15. D. A Producer may not be licensed as a consultant, however, a Producer may act as a consultant if they follow the proper procedures, including full disclosure of the compensation arrangements.

16. C. "Twenty-four in two"

17. D. Changes of address allow the Commissioner to make periodic mailings to Producers. Should a Producer be terminated for cause, the Commissioner will investigate the circumstances.

18. C. The Commissioner may examine any admitted company at any time. The Commissioner must examine all admitted companies at least every five years. However, in the case of a foreign or alien company, where the home state complies with the NAIC examination requirements, the Commissioner may waive the Indiana examination.

19. B. The minimum age for a resident Producer is 18.

© 2017 Pathfinder Corporation

INDIANA LIFE LAW QUIZ

1. Which of the following is the purpose of the Life Insurance Solicitation (Life Insurance Disclosure) regulation?

    (A) To protect policyowners in the event of a life insurance company insolvency.
    (B) To ensure purchasers of life insurance are given enough information to evaluate a policy's cost relative to similar life insurance policies.
    (C) To govern the activities of producers and companies with respect to the replacement of existing life insurance and annuities.
    (D) To standardize the provisions of new forms of life insurance products sold in the state.

2. The insurance company or its producer must provide a prospective life insurance purchaser with a Buyer's Guide and a Policy Summary in which of the following types of life insurance sales?

    (A) Credit Life
    (B) Group Life
    (C) Whole Life
    (D) Variable Life

3. Which of the following statements is NOT true concerning Life Insurance Solicitation statutes and regulations?

    (A) They require that prospective clients be given a Life Insurance Buyer's Guide prepared by the NAIC.
    (B) They require a Policy Summary containing generic insurance information.
    (C) They require life insurance policies contain an unconditional right to return the policy within 10 days from policy delivery for a full refund.
    (D) They are written by the legislature and/or promulgated by the Commissioner.

4. Which of the following is allowed under Rule 39, AIDS Underwriting?

    (A) Requiring AIDS testing as part of the underwriting process.
    (B) Informing the MIB of the presence of HIV antibodies.
    (C) Using the fact that an individual has sought AIDS counseling as an underwriting criteria.
    (D) Providing lower benefits for AIDS-related losses than other claims.

© 2017 Pathfinder Corporation

5. Under Rule 48, all of the following may trigger Accelerated Death Benefits EXCEPT

   (A)   Terminal illness.
   (B)   Permanent institutionalization.
   (C)   A medical condition that will drastically shorten the insured's life.
   (D)   Total disability.

6. Under Indiana Law

   (A)   Accelerated Death Benefits must be taken as a lump sum.
   (B)   Companies must waive further premium after the payment of Accelerated Death Benefits.
   (C)   There are no restrictions on the discount rates for Accelerated Death Benefits.
   (D)   Accelerated Death Benefits which have been paid act as a lien against the death benefit.

7. Viatical Settlement Contracts can also be referred to as

   (A)   Viators.
   (B)   Accelerated Death Benefits.
   (C)   Living Benefit Agreements.
   (D)   Section 403(b) Annuities.

8. Producer Bart makes a sales presentation to Betty for a Universal Life policy. While completing the application, Bart learns that Betty is insured under a life policy. Bart must give Betty the Important Notice Regarding the Replacement of Life Insurance and a copy of the Sales Proposal used in the presentation under all of the following situations EXCEPT

   (A)   Betty tells Bart that she will exchange her original policy for a reduced paid-up policy.
   (B)   Betty decides to follow Bart's recommendation that she continue her Whole Life as extended term insurance.
   (C)   Betty says that coming up with the initial premium for the UL will not be a problem as she will borrow all the cash value out of her existing policy to pay it.
   (D)   Betty will convert her existing Convertible Term policy to Whole Life.

9.   Which of the following is the intent of the Replacement regulation?

(A)   To limit the number of times replacement may occur.
(B)   To protect existing insurers from having policies replaced by
       producers representing companies with inferior life insurance policies.
(C)   To determine the penalties if producers or companies fail to comply
       with the Replacement regulation.
(D)   To assure that the client is given enough information to make a
       decision in his or her own best interest.

10.   Linda is purchasing a new Universal Life policy. Replacement would be
      involved in all of the following situations EXCEPT

(A)   Linda will terminate an existing Term to Age 65 policy.
(B)   Linda will place an existing Whole Life policy on Extended Term.
(C)   Linda will allow a one-year Term policy to expire.
(D)   Linda will borrow 35% of the cash value of her existing Whole Life
       policy to purchase the new Universal Life policy.

11.   Under a Viatical Settlement agreement, the insured person is known as the

(A)   Viatical
(B)   Viator
(C)   Beneficiary
(D)   Third party

12   All of the following are benefits which can be paid under an Accelerated
      Death benefit EXCEPT

(A)   Dread Disease
(B)   Total Disability
(C)   Terminal Illness
(D)   Nursing Home

13.   Joe sells his policy to a Viatical Company. All of the following are true
      EXCEPT

(A)   Joe has been diagnosed with a terminal illness.
(B)   Joe will receive the face amount of his life insurance policy from the
       Viatical company.
(C)   Joe will assign ownership of his policy to the Viatical company.
(D)   Joe must be mentally competent.

© 2017 PATHFINDER Corporation

14. The primary difference between Viatical Settlements and Accelerated Death benefits is that

(A) Viaticals require an extra premium, whereas Accelerated Death Benefits do not.
(B) Viaticals can be used to fund retirement, whereas Accelerated Death Benefits cannot.
(C) Viaticals are funded by a third party, whereas in an Accelerated Death Benefit, the proceeds come from the company that issued the original policy.
(D) Viaticals are not regulated by the Department of Insurance.

END

QUIZ ANSWERS & EXPLANATIONS ON NEXT PAGE

© 2017 Pathfinder Corporation

INDIANA LIFE LAW QUIZ ANSWER KEY

1. B. The purpose of this regulation is indeed to allow consumers enough information to compare "apples with apples." There is a separate regulation dealing with Replacement.

2. C. The Solicitation regulation does not apply to Group or Credit insurance. As a security, Variable Life products are subject to stiffer regulations. The correct answer is indeed Whole Life.

3. B. The Buyer's Guide contains generic information; the Policy Summary contains information about the specific policy. The remaining statements are true.

4. A. AIDS testing may be used in underwriting, as it is relevant to assessing risk. The seeking of counseling itself does not establish an increased risk. The Rule also prohibits transmitting information concerning HIV, and does not allow reduced benefits for AIDS-related claims.

5. D. Total disability alone will not trigger an Accelerated Death Benefit. The threshold is terminal illness, a life shortening condition, or one which requires extraordinary medical care or permanent institutionalization.

6. D. As Accelerated Death Benefits need not be taken as a lump sum, the company can indeed charge premium for any benefits remaining under the contract. The amount of the "discount" is regulated. Finally, any benefits paid out under the Accelerated Death Benefit act as a lien against the Death Benefit (You cannot have your cake and eat it too).

7. C. Viatical Settlements, a contract between the insured and a third party purchaser, may be referred to as Living Benefit Agreements.

8. D. Replacement takes place whenever any value of an existing policy is significantly diminished. In A, the death benefit is reduced; in B, the cash value is eliminated; in C, any policy loan that exceeds 25% of the cash value triggers Replacement. No value is diminished in D, hence no replacement.

© 2017 Pathfinder Corporation

INDIANA LIFE LAW QUIZ ANSWER KEY

9.   D.   The spirit of the Replacement Regulation is disclosure. The consumer must receive enough information to make an intelligent choice regarding replacement of an existing policy.

10.   C.   Allowing an existing Term policy to expire is not replacement. The remaining instances all involve the diminishing of some policy value.

11.   B.   The viator is the insured--the viatical is another way of referring to the purchase contract itself.

12.   B.   Remember that disability itself is not covered under the regulation, more stringent conditions must exist.

13.   B.   In order to enter the contract, as with any other contact, the viator must be competent. There must be a terminal diagnosis. The Living Benefit Agreement transfers ownership to the purchaser. Joe will not receive full value, but a discounted value. The depth of the discount will depend on Joe's prognosis, i.e., his life expectancy.

14.   C.   Viatical Settlements involve the purchase of the rights to benefits, at a discount, by a third party. The original carrier, on the other hand, provides Accelerated Death Benefits, either as part of the policy itself, or as a rider.

© 2017 Pathfinder Corporation

INDIANA HEALTH LAW QUIZ

1. Under Indiana Law, all of the following are true regarding the Relation to Earnings Provision EXCEPT

    (A) The minimum benefit allowed is $200 per month.
    (B) There can be a pro rata refund of unearned premium for up to 2 years.
    (C) The provision, while not mandatory itself, must be offered with every Disability Income policy.
    (D) The provision affects those individuals whose actual earnings are less than the benefits promised in their Disability Income policies.

2. The Indiana statute regarding pre-existing conditions limitations in individual Health Insurance policies

    (A) Applies to both Accident and Health contracts and Long Term Care policies.
    (B) Has a maximum limitation period of 12 months.
    (C) Is limited only to those conditions for which treatment was actually received.
    (D) Has a maximum limitation period equal to the elimination period found in the policy.

3. The purpose of the Indiana Comprehensive Health Insurance Association is to

    (A) Replace Medicaid.
    (B) Protect those who are covered by insolvent insurers.
    (C) Provide Health Insurance for those who cannot acquire coverage, at a reasonable cost, through normal channels.
    (D) Supplement the benefits provided under Medicare.

4. All of the following are excluded under ICHIA policies EXCEPT

    (A) Workers Comp claims
    (B) Custodial Care
    (C) Elective Cosmetic surgery
    (D) AIDS

© 2017 Pathfinder Corporation

5.   The primary purpose of the LTCP program is to

(A)   Provide LTC benefits which will not be covered by Medicare.
(B)   Allow for the sheltering of assets from the Medicaid spend down.
(C)   Allow for LTC Coverage to be written in days rather than dollars provided as benefits.
(D)   Act as a pool, providing coverage for substandard LTC risks.

6.   All of the following are true regarding education requirements for producers selling LTC products under Indiana law EXCEPT

(A)   All producers selling LTC products must have a minimum of 8 hours of approved post licensing education.
(B)   All producers selling LTCP products must have a minimum of 15 hours of approved post licensing education.
(C)   All producers selling LTC products must dedicate a portion of their ConEd hours to approved LTC ConEd courses.
(D)   Those producers holding a limited LTC license must take all 10 of their required ConEd hours as approved LTC courses.

7.   All of the following are true regarding LTCP coverages EXCEPT

(A)   Inflation protection, while not mandatory, must be offered with every policy.
(B)   Benefits must be expressed in dollars.
(C)   The minimum inflation protections may be based on an annual percentage increase or be attached to the CPI.
(D)   They must allow for proportionate increases in maximum benefit levels.

8.   Under the Coordination of Benefits clause in group A&H, the policy which pays first is referred to as the

(A)   Qualifying Coverage
(B)   Preferred Provider
(C)   Primary Coverage
(D)   Payor Benefit

9. In coordinating A&H Benefits, under Rule 38.1, the children's medical expenses will be

   (A) Split pro-rata by the carriers of each parent.
   (B) Split equally by the carriers of each parent.
   (C) Paid primarily by the carrier of the parent with the highest earned income.
   (D) Paid primarily by the parent whose birthday falls first in the calendar year.

10. Under the Indiana Small Group Statute, a small group is defined as one

    (A) Where all employees are working at a single location.
    (B) With less than 100 members.
    (C) That complies with Subchapter S of the Internal Revenue Service Code.
    (D) With between 2 and 50 employees.

11. Under the Indiana Small Group Statute, which of the following would be a late enrollee?

    (A) An individual who lost other coverage because of termination of employment.
    (B) An individual who lost other coverage because of death.
    (C) An individual who decided to buy coverage because of the birth of a child.
    (D) An individual who lost coverage because of dissolution of marriage.

12. Under the Indiana Small Group Statute, the maximum preexisting conditions period for late enrollees is

    (A) 6 months
    (B) 12 months
    (C) 15 months
    (D) 24 months

13. Under the Small Group Statute, a dependent child who loses coverage due to their parents' divorce will not be considered a late enrollee if coverage is requested within:

    (A) 10 days
    (B) 20 days
    (C) 30 days
    (D) 45 days

© 2017 Pathfinder Corporation

INDIANA HEALTH LAW QUIZ

14. Joe and Jolene both work and are both insured under Group Major Medical plans by their employers. Both plans also cover dependent children. If Joe and Jolene get divorced, which of the following is true about coverage for the children?

(A) Jolene's plan will be primary if her birthday comes before Joe's birthday in the year.

(B) If Joe and Jolene have the same birthdate, then the plan that has been in effect the longest will be primary.

(C) The plan of the parent who is the subject of the support order shall be primary.

(D) None of the above.

END

QUIZ ANSWERS & EXPLANATIONS ON NEXT PAGE

INDIANA HEALH LAW QUIZ ANSWER KEY

1. C. While the Relation to Earnings Provision is an optional provision under the NAIC Model Provisions, it is mandatory under Indiana law.

2. B. The 12-month limit applies only to individual policies--preexisting conditions in Group Medical Expense policies are regulated by federal law (HIPAA). In individual policies, preexisting conditions include "any condition for which a reasonable person would have sought treatment."

3. C. ICHIA is a pool that spreads substandard health risks among the health carriers doing business in Indiana; the result is lower premium for those who could not afford coverage through normal channels. ICHIA does not replace Medicaid as there are no income limitations for insureds. The Guaranty Association protects those covered by insolvent insurers.

4. D. AIDS benefits are not excluded under ICHIA. The others are excluded as being "better covered elsewhere."

5. B. The LTCP program allows insureds to shelter an amount equal to the policy benefits from the Medicaid "spend down."

6. D. There is no such thing as a "limited LTC license." Persons selling LTC must have a Health license with an LTC certification (an 8 hour requirement); those selling LTCP policies must have an additional 7 hours of education, (for a total of 15 hours.) Producers with the LTC certification must also dedicate a portion of their ConEd to LTC.

7. A. While inflation protection is optional in a standard LTC policy, it is mandatory in an LTCP policy.

8. C. The Primary Coverage pays before the Secondary Coverage.

9. D. Indiana follows the "first birthday" rule for Coordination of Benefits.

10. D. A small group has between 2 and 50 members.

11. C. Late enrollees are ones who failed to purchase coverage of their own accord.

12. C. 15 months is the correct answer.

© 2017 Pathfinder Corporation

INDIANA HEALTH LAW QUIZ ANSWER KEY

13.   C.   The time limit is 30 days.

14.   C.   The first birthday rule does not apply in the case of divorce. The plan of the parent who is the subject of the support order shall be primary.

© 2017 Pathfinder Corporation

CHAPTERS 1 - 3
CONTRACT LAW & UNDERWRITING

1.   Insurance policies normally define a representation as

   (A)   A statement that must be absolutely true.
   (B)   A statement that must be true to the best of the applicant's knowledge and belief.
   (C)   A statement made in writing on an application.
   (D)   An oral contract.

2.   To protect the insuring public, in order to apply for insurance on someone else's life, an applicant must have which of the following?

   (A)   An insurable interest in the life of the proposed insured at the time of application.
   (B)   The proposed insured's help in completing the application.
   (C)   An insurable interest in the life of the proposed insured throughout the term of the policy.
   (D)   The proposed insured's written consent as well as an insurable interest in his or her life at the time of application.

3.   Which of the following is true about incomplete applications for Life and Health insurance?

   (A)   An incomplete application should be returned to the customer by the producer for completion and be initialed next to the changes made.
   (B)   Incomplete applications that are forwarded to an insurance company will be completed by the underwriter by calling the applicant for the answers to the questions.
   (C)   A policy issued on the basis of an incomplete application will be null and void at the end of the contestable period.
   (D)   An incomplete application must be destroyed and a new application must be completed by the applicant.

© 2017 Pathfinder Corporation

CHAPTERS 1-3 • CONTRACT LAW & UNDERWRITING QUIZ

4. Producer Larry Lax takes an application from a proposed insured without any premium. Legally, the application is considered to be

(A) An offer
(B) An invitation to make an offer
(C) A counteroffer
(D) An acceptance

5. Which of the following individuals would NOT sign an application for a Life insurance policy?

(A) The applicant, if different than proposed insured.
(B) The proposed insured.
(C) The actuary.
(D) The Producer.

6. Which of the following is the effective date of coverage for an applicant who has been issued a Conditional Receipt for a life insurance policy?

(A) The date the Producer receives the policy from the insurance company.
(B) The date the Producer accepts the prepaid application.
(C) The date the insurance company's home office receives the application and the applicant's medical information.
(D) The date of the application or the date of the medical examination, whichever is later, if the applicant is insurable as applied for.

7. Insurance is considered to be in force when the

(A) Producer completes the application and the proposed insured signs it.
(B) Proposed insured signs an application and a medical examiner acceptable to the insurance company completes an examination of the proposed insured.
(C) Agency manager deposits the initial premium check into an escrow account.
(D) Insurance company mails a policy to the Producer, the Producer delivers it to the proposed insured, collects the first premium, and obtains a signed statement of continued good health.

8.   The Fair Credit Reporting Act provides

   (A)   That the applicant for insurance be informed that a consumer report may be requested.
   (B)   Protection to debtors against harassment by lending institutions in the event of default.
   (C)   For the availability of Credit Life insurance on a fair and impartial basis.
   (D)   The funding for a national clearinghouse of credit information for life insurance company underwriting operations.

9.   All the following are characteristics of insurance contracts EXCEPT that they are

   (A)   Contracts of adhesion.
   (B)   Aleatory contracts.
   (C)   Conditional contracts.
   (D)   Bi-lateral contracts.

10.   All of the following relationships normally indicate the presence of insurable interest EXCEPT

   (A)   A bank insuring the life of a customer in the amount of his savings account balance.
   (B)   A wife insuring the life of her husband.
   (C)   An employee insuring the life of his employer to provide funding for a business purchase agreement.
   (D)   An individual insuring her own life.

11.   On June 1, B submitted an application for a life insurance policy, and was issued a conditional receipt. On June 6, B took the required medical exam. On June 20, the company issued the policy as applied for and on June 25, the Producer, when delivering the policy, discovers that B died on June 18. Which of the following is true?

   (A)   There is no coverage because B died before the policy was delivered.
   (B)   The insurance company must return the premiums paid to insured's estate because there will not be coverage.
   (C)   The insurer must pay the death benefit to the designated beneficiary.
   (D)   The insurance company will pay 80% of the death benefit because the insured died prior to signing the Statement of Continued Good Health.

© 2017 Pathfinder Corporation

12. To be insurable, a risk must be all the following EXCEPT:

(A) Measurable in dollars.
(B) Economically significant to the applicant.
(C) Predictable in size so rates can be established by the insurer.
(D) A certainty.

13. On June 19, an application and the initial premium were taken from a prospective insured for a standard rate policy, and a conditional receipt was issued. However, the applicant was only approved on a substandard basis by the insurance company on June 26, and a rated policy was issued on June 27. The policy was delivered to and accepted by the applicant on July 1, and the additional premium was paid. On what date did coverage become effective?

(A) June 19
(B) June 26
(C) June 27
(D) July 1

14. You take a life insurance application on Harvey Anderson. Three weeks later, the policy is issued and you deliver it to him at his home. Five weeks after delivery of the policy, Harvey dies. Shortly after Harvey's death, the insurance company notices that several questions were not answered on the application for the policy. What will the company do?

(A) Return the premium paid.
(B) Sue Harvey's estate on the basis of concealment of material information.
(C) Obtain the missing information and determine the appropriate action.
(D) Pay the claim.

15.   American Mutual Insurance Company received an application and premium payment for a policy on Joe Insured on May 5. On May 8, a Medical Information Bureau report obtained by American Mutual showed that Joe recently had a heart attack which would render him uninsurable. This information, however, was not disclosed on his application. Which of the following actions would American Mutual probably NOT take?

(A)   Forward to Joe a copy of his MIB report.
(B)   Return Joe's premium to him.
(C)   Refuse to issue the policy as applied for.
(D)   Tell the Producer that Joe was denied coverage.

16.   Which of the following statements about underwriting selection is true?

(A)   Insurance companies may use family history to rate an applicant if that history reveals a characteristic which might also appear in the applicant.
(B)   An applicant is always required to pay the first year's premium at the time she applies for insurance.
(C)   Adverse selection is the tendency of good risks to purchase insurance.
(D)   The Law of Large Numbers has been repealed.

17.   Which of the following is true about a prepaid application for Life or Health insurance?

(A)   The insurance company is always bound to the risk once its Producer accepts a prepaid application from a proposed insured.
(B)   An insurance company is bound to issue the policy as applied for if the Producer issues a conditional receipt to the applicant.
(C)   The insurance company is never bound to a risk until the Producer has manually delivered the policy to the proposed insured.
(D)   The insurance company is bound to the risk if the policy is manually delivered to the proposed insured by the Producer and there has been no substantial change in the proposed insured's health since the time of application.

18. Which of the following legal terms refers to the fact that in a life insurance agreement only one of the two parties makes any promises?

   (A) Adhesion
   (B) Unilateral
   (C) Estoppel
   (D) Conditional

19. Which of the following is an insurance industry association organized and operated to collect and disseminate medical information to its member companies?

   (A) NAIC
   (B) NASD
   (C) Fair Credit Reporting
   (D) MIB

20. Dividends paid by Mutual companies are

   (A) Guaranteed
   (B) Taxed
   (C) A return of overcharge
   (D) None of the above

21. Insurance contracts may result in an unequal exchange of consideration between the insurer and the insured. Therefore the contract is said to be

   (A) An aleatory contract.
   (B) An obligatory contract.
   (C) A contract of varying value.
   (D) A reciprocal contract.

22. If there is a legal ambiguity in the wording of a life insurance policy, the court will

   (A) Declare that the insurer is correct and cancel the policy.
   (B) Allow the insurer to raise the premium to cover any increased risk.
   (C) State that the policy is a contract of adhesion and that the burden of proof is therefore on the insured.
   (D) Find for the insured as insurance policies are contracts of adhesion.

© 2017 Pathfinder Corporation

23. Which of the following is true concerning AIDS testing and underwriting?

(A) A company may require an AIDS test of anyone who discloses that he or she has previously sought AIDS testing.

(B) No specific permission is required for a company to conduct AIDS/HIV testing on an applicant.

(C) If one company's blood test reveals the presence of AIDS antibodies, other companies will have access to this knowledge through the MIB.

(D) A policy may not contain exclusions for AIDS/HIV losses.

24. With a Conditional Receipt, the earliest that coverage can begin is:

(A) The date of the Conditional Receipt.

(B) The date the policy is approved.

(C) The date of the physical exam.

(D) The date the policy is delivered.

25. All of the following are valid underwriting considerations EXCEPT:

(A) A dangerous vocation such as firefighter.

(B) A dangerous avocation such as mountain climber.

(C) The fact the applicant is male.

(D) The race of the applicant.

END

QUIZ ANSWERS & EXPLANATIONS ON NEXT PAGE

© 2017 Pathfinder Corporation

CHAPTERS 1 - 3
CONTRACT LAW & UNDERWRITING ANSWER KEY

1. B. A representation is a written or oral statement that the insured believes to be true.

2. D. Both consent of the insured and insurable interest are required to purchase a policy on the life of another.

3. A. Incomplete applications must be returned to the customer by the producer and all required questions answered.

4. B. Application without premium is an Invitation to Make an Offer. An application with premium is an offer.

5. C. There is no requirement for an actuary to sign an application.

6. D. With a Conditional Receipt, coverage begins on the later of the application date or physical exam date, if the policy is issued as applied for.

7. D. Coverage begins when required premium has been paid, the policy is physically delivered and a statement of continued good health is obtained.

8. A. Applicants must be advised that a consumer report (credit report) may be requested.

9. D. Insurance contracts are Unilateral Contracts; meaning only one party (the insurance company) makes legally enforceable promises.

10. A. A bank has no reasonable expectation that they will get to keep the money in a savings account. Therefore, the bank has no insurable interest on a savings account.

11. C. With a Conditional Receipt, coverage begins on the later of the application date or physical exam date, if the policy is issued as applied for. In this case, the policy effective date was June 6. When B died, insurance was in force and the company must pay the death benefit.

© 2017 Pathfinder Corporation

CHAPTERS 1-3
CONTRACT LAW & UNDERWRITING QUIZ ANSWER KEY

12.   D.   Risk is a chance of loss. Insurance companies would not want to insure something where they knew a loss would happen for certain.

13.   D.   Because the insured was substandard risk the policy was not issued as applied for and a counter-offer was made. Coverage begins when and if the insured accepts the counter-offer. In this case coverage begins on July 1.

14.   D.   The insurance company issued a policy based on an application with blank statements. They waived their rights to obtain that information and cannot contest the policy.

15.   A.   If requested, the MIB would forward a copy of sensitive medical files to the insured's doctor, but not to the insured.

16.   A.   Insurance companies can use information concerning certain known genetic conditions in other family members, if such conditions could appear in the applicant.

17.   D.   The insurance company is bound to the risk when they accept a legal offer. Acceptance can be through Interim Insuring agreements or when the policy is physically delivered.

18.   B.   Insurance contracts are Unilateral Contracts; meaning only one party (the insurance company) makes legally enforceable promises.

19.   D.   The Medical Information Bureau collects and disseminates medical information.

20.   C.   Dividends from a Mutual Company are never guaranteed or taxed. They are simply a return of unneeded premium.

21.   A.   Insurance contracts are Aleatory contracts because they will never benefit the insured and the insurance company equally.

22.   D.   The company writes the entire contract and is therefore stuck to what they have written. Any ambiguity or confusion in the contract would be settled in favor of the insured.

© 2017 Pathfinder Corporation

CHAPTERS 1-3
CONTRACT LAW & UNDERWRITING QUIZ ANSWER KEY

23.   D.   AIDS/HIV cannot be excluded in a Life contract. The MIB would only be made aware of certain abnormalities in a blood test, but they would not be informed of the presence of HIV antibodies.

24.   A.   With a Conditional Receipt coverage begins on the later of the application date or physical exam date, if the policy is issued as applied for. The date of the Conditional Receipt would be the same as the date of application.

25.   D.   Age, sex, hobbies, and your job can be considered, but race can never be considered in underwriting.

© 2017 Pathfinder Corporation

CHAPTER 4
LIFE INSURANCE & ANNUITIES

1. When an insured purchases a Decreasing Term policy, which of the following decreases each year?

    (A)   The interest rate
    (B)   The premium
    (C)   The face amount
    (D)   The cash value

2. At age 30, Jolene Insured bought a Whole Life policy and has paid the premiums as agreed for 10 years. Now, at age 40, the policy's cash value is

    (A)   A function of the profitability of her company.
    (B)   Largely determined by Jolene's health at age 40.
    (C)   A function of the investment return enjoyed by her company over the last 10 years.
    (D)   The amount that was guaranteed in the contract when she purchased it at age 30.

3. A Term policy is designed to mature upon which of the following?

    (A)   The death of the insured during the insured period.
    (B)   The insured's attainment of age 100.
    (C)   The date of policy expiration.
    (D)   When the insured turns age 65.

4. A traditional Whole Life policy is designed to mature upon all of the following EXCEPT:

    (A)   The death of the insured during the insured period.
    (B)   The insured's attainment of age 100.
    (C)   The end of the premium payment period.
    (D)   When the cash value equals the face amount.

© 2017 Pathfinder Corporation

CHAPTER 4 • LIFE INSURANCE & ANNUITIES QUIZ

5. Which of the following is NOT normally considered a personal use of life insurance?

    (A) Survivor protection
    (B) Disability Income benefits
    (C) Estate creation
    (D) Liquidity

6. Which of the following contracts is primarily designed to provide a series of benefit payments at regular intervals following retirement throughout the lifetime of one or more persons?

    (A) Convertible Term
    (B) Life Annuity
    (C) Annuity Certain
    (D) Whole Life

Questions 7 through 9 are based upon the following circumstances:

At age 40, Joe Insured decided to buy an insurance policy in the amount of $100,000. He considered four policies marketed by Swineherds Mutual.

    (A) 20-Pay Life
    (B) Life Paid at 65
    (C) 20-Year Endowment
    (D) Annually Renewable Term to age 65

Choose from the policies listed above the one that is best described by the following. A policy form may be used once, more than once or not at all.

7. The policy which will have the lowest annual premium in the first policy year.

    (A)   (B)   (C)   (D)

8. The policy which will guarantee protection for Joe Insured until age 100 and develop cash value at the fastest rate.

    (A)   (B)   (C)   (D)

CHAPTER 4 • LIFE INSURANCE & ANNUITIES QUIZ

9. The policy whose premium will increase each year.

   (A)   (B)   (C)   (D)

10. Which of the following would NOT be a common use of annuities?

    (A) To provide a life income.
    (B) To provide funds for retirement.
    (C) To take advantage of tax deferred growth.
    (D) To provide a death benefit not subject to the federal income tax.

11. Any life insurance policy whose cash value grows faster than a 7 Pay Whole Life policy is considered a(n):

    (A) Whole Life
    (B) Endowment
    (C) Joint and 2/3 Survivorship Life Annuity with Period Certain
    (D) Modified Endowment

12. The principal use of a Life Annuity is to

    (A) Create capital for the annuitant's heirs.
    (B) Provide for the liquidation of the annuitant's debts at retirement.
    (C) Provide capital for the annuitant's beneficiary.
    (D) Provide an income for the annuitant's retirement.

13. Joe College purchases a Renewable and Convertible Level Term policy. Three years later when he converts the policy to Whole Life, his premium increases. This could be due to which of the following?

    (A) The Whole Life premiums are based upon his attained age at conversion.
    (B) The interest rate paid on the general account may have declined during the 3 year period.
    (C) The insured's health may have declined.
    (D) The insured may have changed to a higher risk occupation.

© 2017 Pathfinder Corporation

14. Federal income tax laws generally treat the death benefits paid from life insurance policies as

(A) Taxable as ordinary income.
(B) Tax deferred.
(C) Not taxable as income to the beneficiary.
(D) Taxable as long term capital gains above the cost basis.

15. Which of the following annuities would provide an income for Joe and Jolene for as long as either one of them is alive?

(A) A Life Annuity with Period Certain
(B) A Refund Life Annuity
(C) A Joint and Survivor Life Annuity
(D) An Immediate Annuity

16. Which of the following is NOT true concerning fixed annuities?

(A) If the policyowner dies during the accumulation period, the cash value of the account or the premium paid, whichever is higher, is returned to the annuitant's heirs/beneficiaries.
(B) At the end of the accumulation period, the annuitant has the option of surrendering the contract for its cash value rather than annuitizing the contract.
(C) During the income phase of a Joint and Survivor Life Annuity, when the first annuitant dies, a lump sum is paid to the surviving spouse.
(D) All other things being equal, a male annuitant would receive a higher monthly amount during the annuity period than a female annuitant.

17. Ann, at age 45, purchased a contract with a single premium of $50,000. The contract will accumulate earnings on a tax deferred basis until Ann is age 65, at which point she will receive a monthly income for the remainder of her life. The amount of the monthly benefit on pay-out will fluctuate according to the contract's underlying investments. Which of the following statements is NOT true regarding the contract Ann has purchased?

(A) Ann purchased a Single Premium Retirement Annuity.
(B) Ann owns a Variable Annuity.
(C) Ann owns a Conventional Life Annuity With 20-Year Certain.
(D) If Ann dies at age 66 after having received only a portion of the total cash accumulated, the income benefit will cease.

© 2017 Pathfinder Corporation

CHAPTER 4 • LIFE INSURANCE & ANNUITIES QUIZ

18. At age 65 you purchase a Single Premium Immediate Life Annuity with 10-Year Period Certain. Which of the following statements is true?

   (A) The annuity will pay an income for a period of time not to exceed 10 years.
   (B) The annuity will pay an income for as long as you live, but in no event less than 10 years.
   (C) The annuity will pay an income for the rest of your life, but if you die within the next 10 years the income will stop upon your death.
   (D) You will start receiving an income benefit at age 75 for a period of 10 years.

19. Which of the following annuity pay out systems guarantees the return of at least all of the principal invested in the policy?

   (A) Joint and Survivorship Life Annuity
   (B) Cash Refund Life Annuity
   (C) Life Annuity with Period Certain
   (D) Straight Life Annuity

20. Which of the following annuities would have the principal invested in the separate account rather than in the general account?

   (A) Annuity Certain
   (B) Fixed Annuity
   (C) Variable Annuity
   (D) Deferred Annuity

21. Which of the following is NOT true concerning the taxation of an annuity?

   (A) The earnings of the invested monies are tax deferred until they are withdrawn.
   (B) Monies withdrawn from the annuity prior to age 59 1/2 may be subject to a penalty tax.
   (C) Monies received during the pay-out phase are taxed as ordinary income above the cost basis.
   (D) The death benefits received are free from federal income tax.

© 2017 Pathfinder Corporation

22. An annuity in which the payout amount will never fluctuate is a (an):

(A)   Joint and 2/3 Life Annuity.
(B)   Fixed, conventional Life Annuity.
(C)   Indexed Life Annuity.
(D)   Variable Life Annuity.

23. All of the following statements concerning an Annuity are true EXCEPT:

(A)   Annuity payouts on a life annuity are based on the age and sex of the annuitant at the time the payout begins.
(B)   Interest dollars earned during the accumulation phase of an annuity are not taxed until withdrawn.
(C)   Premature distributions from an annuity will be subject to income taxes and a 20% penalty.
(D)   Annuities may be purchased with a single premium.

24. Annuities can best be described as

(A)   A substitute for life insurance.
(B)   A tax free retirement vehicle.
(C)   A reasonable alternative to purchasing a disability income policy.
(D)   The systematic liquidation of an estate.

25. An Immediate Annuity has no accumulation period which means it can only be purchased

(A)   With a level premium.
(B)   With a flexible premium.
(C)   Within 30 days of the annuitant's 65th birthday.
(D)   With a single premium.

26. A single premium Whole Life policy will:

(A)   Experience a slower growth of cash value.
(B)   Mature sooner.
(C)   Be considered paid-up immediately.
(D)   Expire at age 65.

© 2017 Pathfinder Corporation

27.   Changes can be made by the policyowner of an annuity:

(A)   Only during the income phase.
(B)   Only during the accumulation phase.
(C)   Only when there is a verifiable change in health.
(D)   During the pay-in or pay-out phase.

END

QUIZ ANSWERS & EXPLANATIONS ON NEXT PAGE

© 2017 Pathfinder Corporation

CHAPTER 4
LIFE INSURANCE & ANNUITIES
QUIZ ANSWER KEY

1.   C.   With Decreasing Term, it is the face amount (death benefit) of the contract that decreases.

2.   D.   Cash Value is guaranteed in the policy. It does not vary with the company's return on investment, the insured's health, or the actual mortality experience.

3.   A.   Term policies only mature if the insured dies during the term.

4.   C.   Whole Life policies mature in two ways, death or reaching age 100. At age 100 the cash value of the policy will have grown to equal the face amount of the contract.

5.   B.   Disability Income is a health insurance concept. Being disabled does not trigger a payment from a life insurance contract.

6.   B.   A Life Annuity pays benefits for life. An Annuity Certain only pays for a specified period of time or in specified amounts until all the funds in the annuity are depleted.

7.   D.   Term insurance is always the least expensive form of insurance.

8.   A.   The faster the money is paid into a Whole Life policy, the faster the cash value grows. In this case the cash value in a 20 Pay Life contract would grow faster because the money is paid in within 20 years rather than 25 years (Life Paid at 65).

9.   D.   Annually Renewable Term insurance means the policy is renewed on a yearly basis and premiums increase each year.

10.   D.   Annuities never have a death benefit.

11.   D.   By definition.

12.   D.   Life Annuities are primarily designed to provide a life income at retirement.

© 2017 Pathfinder Corporation

13.   A.   When converting a Convertible Term policy, the insured need not prove insurability, so health and occupation concerns could not be reasons for the increased premium.

14.   C.   Death benefits are paid free from Federal Income Tax.

15.   C.   During the income phase of a Joint and Survivor Life Annuity, the annuity will continue to pay as long as either the annuity owner or his spouse (survivor) is alive.

16.   C.   During the income phase of a Joint and Survivor Life Annuity, the annuity will continue to pay as long as either the annuitant or the annuitant's spouse is alive. Monthly benefits are paid, not a lump sum.

17.   C.   There is no guaranteed 20-year period certain in the annuity described.

18.   B.   A Life Annuity with period certain guarantees payment for a limited time whether the annuitant is alive or dead. If the annuitant dies, monthly payments will be made to a beneficiary until the end of the guaranteed period of time. Remember, if the annuitant is still alive, the Life Annuity with Period Certain continues to pay.

19.   B.   A Refund Life Annuity (both Installment Refund and Cash Refund) guarantees that if the annuitant dies before receiving an amount equal to the principal invested, the remaining balance will be paid to a beneficiary.

20.   C.   Variable contacts always utilize a separate investment account.

21.   D.   Annuities have no death benefit.

22.   B.   With fixed dollar, conventional annuities' payouts will not fluctuate.

23.   C.   Premature distributions are subject to taxes and a 10% penalty.

24.   D.   By definition.

25.   D.   Immediate annuities begin paying at once and therefore can only be purchased with a single premium.

26.   C.   A single premium means no more premiums will be required. Therefore, the life policy is all paid-up.

27.   B.   Changes can be made by the owner during the pay-in or accumulation phase, but not during the pay-out or income phase.

CHAPTER 5
LIFE POLICY PROVISIONS

1. A policyowner calls you five years after purchasing a Whole Life policy from you. She tells you that she recently has resigned her job as a schoolteacher and is now working in a more hazardous occupation as a human cannonball in the circus. She wants to know how this change of occupation will affect her insurance policy. You should tell her that

    (A) Her premiums will be increased.
    (B) An aviation rider must be added to the policy.
    (C) A hazardous occupation exclusion will be added to the policy.
    (D) Her premium will be unaffected.

2. Which clause in a life insurance policy contains the insurance company's promises?

    (A) The Consideration Clause.
    (B) The Insuring Clause.
    (C) Santa Clause.
    (D) The Entire Contract/Modifications Clause

3. If you fail to pay your life insurance premium when it is due, which policy provision will initially direct the company's actions?

    (A) Waiver of Premium
    (B) Automatic Premium Loan
    (C) Extended Term
    (D) Grace Period

4. The assignment of a life insurance policy death benefit to a lending institution when obtaining a loan is considered to be what type of assignment?

    (A) Collateral
    (B) Irrevocable
    (C) Contingent
    (D) Absolute

© 2017 Pathfinder Corporation

5. Jolene Insured wishes to name her husband, Joe, as primary beneficiary of her life insurance policy but she wishes to retain all the rights of ownership. Therefore, she should name Joe as a(n)

(A) Tertiary beneficiary.
(B) Revocable beneficiary.
(C) Contingent beneficiary.
(D) Irrevocable beneficiary.

6. Mr. Benny intentionally understates his age on an application for a LIFE policy. Upon his death 10 years later, the company discovers the misstatement. The insurance company will

(A) Pay nothing as Mr. Benny is guilty of fraud.
(B) Pay partial benefits as determined by the premiums actually paid and Mr. Benny's true age.
(C) Pay full benefits as the contestable period has expired.
(D) Return the total premium paid, plus interest, to the beneficiary.

7. A life insurance Policy Loan provision states all of the following EXCEPT:

(A) The policyowner may repay the loan at any time.
(B) The policyowner is charged interest on a policy loan at the rate specified in the policy.
(C) The interest that is not paid when due is added to the loan.
(D) The loan may be for any amount up to the policy's face amount.

8. Mr. Jackson is the owner/insured under a life insurance policy, and Mrs. Jackson is designated as a revocable beneficiary. There are no contingent beneficiaries named. Mrs. Jackson predeceases Mr. Jackson by several years. When Mr. Jackson dies, it is learned that he never changed the beneficiary designation and Mrs. Jackson is still listed as his sole beneficiary. The policy proceeds are payable to

(A) The estate of Mrs. Jackson.
(B) The estate of Mr. Jackson.
(C) The Jackson children.
(D) The heirs designated in Mrs. Jackson's will.

© 2017 Pathfinder Corporation

9.   A life insurance policy is issued with a two year incontestable period. After the two year period, the contract is incontestable for all of the following circumstances EXCEPT:

(A)   An incomplete answer on the application.
(B)   Concealment on the application.
(C)   Material misrepresentation on the application.
(D)   Non-payment of premium.

10.   A life insurance policy which has NOT been surrendered for its cash value may be reinstated by the policyowner at any time within the reinstatement period upon taking all of the following actions EXCEPT:

(A)   Present evidence of insurability of the insured satisfactory to the company.
(B)   Pay all past due premiums with interest.
(C)   Obtain the written consent of any revocable beneficiaries.
(D)   Pay off any outstanding policy loans.

11.   Suppose you own a Whole Life policy with a face value of $100,000 and a cash value of $10,000 and a 6% loan interest rate. You request a maximum loan from the insurance company on an anniversary date and receive $9,400. Which of the following is true?

(A)   The insurance company made a mistake.
(B)   The insurance company retained one year's interest in advance.
(C)   The insurance company never loans the full 100% of the cash value because it is too risky.
(D)   There is a service charge made on all policy loans.

12.   A life insurance policy contains the following clause: The company agrees to pay, subject to the terms and conditions of this policy, the sum insured to the beneficiary immediately upon receipt of due proof of the insured's death.   This clause is known as the

(A)   Insuring Clause
(B)   Entire Contract/Modifications Clause
(C)   Ownership Clause
(D)   Consideration Clause

13. Joe Insured buys a life insurance policy which contains a one year suicide clause and commits suicide three months after receiving his policy. The company will

(A) Pay nothing.
(B) Return the premiums paid.
(C) Return the cash value of the policy.
(D) Pay the full face amount of the policy.

14. Robert Young owns a policy on his own life and names his wife, Loretta, as his sole beneficiary on a revocable basis. They are involved in an aircraft accident in which it is impossible to determine who died first. The benefits are payable in accordance with which of the following?

(A) 100% to Robert's estate.
(B) 100% to Loretta's estate.
(C) 50% to each estate.
(D) 75% to Robert's estate and 25% to Loretta's estate.

15. Mrs. Jones wishes to have the Incontestable Clause in her policy shortened to 6 months. This clause may be shortened by which of the following individuals?

acordado

(A) The Producer
(B) The agency manager
(C) The state sales manager
(D) An executive officer of the company

16. Suppose that you name someone as your irrevocable beneficiary. Without the permission of the irrevocable beneficiary, you give up the right to do all of the following EXCEPT

(A) Change beneficiaries
(B) Borrow against the policy
(C) Surrender the policy and take the cash value
(D) Continue to pay the premium

© 2017 Pathfinder Corporation

17. Joe Insured wishes to name the Buddy Holly Memorial Foundation as the beneficiary of his life policy. Which of the following is true concerning this designation?

    (A) The Foundation cannot be named as it has no insurable interest in Joe's life.

    (B) The Foundation cannot be named without its permission.

    (C) The naming of the Foundation is an example of estoppel.

    (D) Insurance law would permit Joe to make such a designation.

18. A change of beneficiary in an individual life policy can be made by the

    (A) Beneficiary, with the permission of the insured.

    (B) Insured, with the permission of the beneficiary.

    (C) Insured, under all circumstances.

    (D) Policyowner, unless there is an irrevocable beneficiary.

19. Joe Insured purchased a life insurance policy that went into effect on the first day of May. Five days after delivery of the policy, Joe returned the policy to the issuing insurance company for a full refund of premium. A week later Joe died. If Jolene submits a claim for the death benefit to the company, the company will do which of the following?

    (A) Pay the claim because the policy was still in force under the grace period provision at the time of Joe's death.

    (B) Pay the claim but deduct the premium due for the period of time the policy was in force.

    (C) Deny the claim as the contract was rescinded.

    (D) Pay the claim because Joe had died before the company had returned the premium to him.

20. Beneficiary designation options could include

    (A) Minors

    (B) Trusts

    (C) Estates

    (D) All the above

© 2017 Pathfinder Corporation

21.   At age 80, Joe is a widower with two adult children who have children of their own. Joe wants the benefits of his policy to go to his two children. If one of them predeceases Joe, he wants that half of his benefits to go to the deceased child's family. He should name his children as beneficiaries on what basis?

    (A)   Per Diem
    (B)   Per Capita
    (C)   Per Stirpes
    (D)   Per Annum

22.   Joe dies owing ABC Loan Company $10,000. His Life policy has a death benefit of $100,000, payable to Joe Jr. The policy contains a Spendthrift Clause. Which of the following is true?

    (A)   ABC can attach the death benefit in the amount of $10,000.
    (B)   ABC cannot attach the death benefit in the amount of $10,000.
    (C)   ABC can attach only if the benefits are paid in a lump sum.
    (D)   None of the above.

23.   An insurance company's challenge to an application is limited by:

    (A)   Errors and Omissions
    (B)   The Incontestable Clause
    (C)   Company guidelines
    (D)   The Fair Credit Reporting Act

END

QUIZ ANSWERS & EXPLANATIONS ON NEXT PAGE

© 2017 Pathfinder Corporation

CHAPTER 5
LIFE POLICY PROVISIONS QUIZ ANSWER KEY

1. D. The insurance company cannot use change of occupation as justification to increase premiums. With a Whole Life policy premiums are guaranteed never to increase.

2. B. The Insuring Clause contains the company's consideration (its promise to pay).

3. D. The Grace Period Clause specifies how long the policyowner has to pay the premium after it is due. If the policyowner/insured dies during the Grace Period the death benefit will be paid, minus the overdue premium.

4. A. A Collateral or Temporary Assignment is used to secure a loan from a financial institution. Once the loan is repaid all ownership rights revert to the policyowner.

5. B. Naming the beneficiary as revocable means that the policyowner has not relinquished any rights of ownership.

6. B. The Misstatement of Age and Sex Clause allows the insurance company to adjust the death benefit based on the true information.

7. D. The Policy Loan cannot exceed the cash value in the policy.

8. B. If all revocable beneficiaries have died before the policyowner/insured, the death benefit will be paid to the policyowner's estate. He who dies last, wins.

9. D. Statements on the application cannot be contested beyond the contestable period. However, not paying the premium could cause the policy to lapse and no death benefit would be paid under those circumstances.

10. C. A revocable beneficiary does not need to consent to reinstatement.

11. B. Interest is charged on policy loans. The first year's interest in charged in advance.

12. A. The Insuring Clause contains the company's consideration (its promise to pay).

13. B. If the insured commits suicide during the suicide exclusion period, premiums paid will be refunded. Suicide after the exclusion period will result in the death benefit being paid.

14. A. The Uniform Simultaneous Death Act specifies that if the policyowner/insured and the beneficiary die in the same occurrence, and it's impossible to determine who died first, the death benefit will be paid to the estate of the insured.

15. D. Only an executive officer of the insurance company can make changes to a policy.

16. D. Essentially, if a policyowner names a beneficiary on an irrevocable basis it means they relinquish most of their ownership rights. However, they still have the right to pay the premium.

17. D. Insurance law permits the policyowner to name any beneficiary they choose.

18. D. The policyowner has the right to name and change beneficiaries. However, if there is an irrevocable beneficiary, no changes can be made without the permission of the irrevocable beneficiary.

19. C. Joe took advantage of the Free Look Provision to return his policy for a refund of premium. Once he returned the policy the policy is considered rescinded. It's as if the policy never existed. When he dies a week later, there is no policy and therefore no death benefit.

20. D. Minors can be beneficiaries, although there must be a guardian appointed. Trusts and estates call also be beneficiaries.

21. C. Per Stirpes means the death benefit will follow along bloodlines and will be split among surviving children and the family of a deceased child.

22. B. Creditors of the insured cannot attach (seek to be paid from) the death benefit, with or without a Spendthrift Clause.

23. B. The insurance company can only contest statements on an application for a limited amount of time. The amount of time is always stated in the Incontestable Clause.

CHAPTER 6
LIFE POLICY OPTIONS

1. Under the Accumulate at Interest dividend option, which of the following is true about the taxation of the interest earned on reinvested dividends?

    ganado

    (A) The interest on the dividends is tax deferred until the money is withdrawn from the account.
    (B) The interest earned on the dividends is tax free.
    (C) The interest on the dividends is taxable in the year in which the interest is earned.
    (D) The interest earned on the dividends is tax sheltered just as the interest earned on the cash value is sheltered.

    protegido

2. L owns a participating Life insurance policy. All of the following statements are true regarding L's policy EXCEPT:

    (A) Policy dividends can be used to shorten the payment period.
    (B) Cash dividends received by L are not subject to income tax.
    (C) If L does not choose a dividend option, the automatic option that will be selected by the insurance company is the Paid Up Additions option.
    (D) L's dividends are guaranteed.

Questions 3 through 6 refer to the following situation.

Mr. Z purchases a $100,000 Continuous Premium Whole Life policy at age 20. At age 40, he no longer wishes to make premium payments.

3. If he stops paying premiums and fails to select a nonforfeiture option, the option automatically assigned by his company would be which of the following?

    (A) Cash
    (B) Reduced Paid-Up
    (C) Extended Term
    (D) Convertible Term

© 2017 Pathfinder Corporation

4. If he selects to surrender the policy for cash, he will receive which of the following?

   (A) The face amount of the policy.
   (B) An amount equal to premiums paid with interest and accumulated dividends.
   (C) The cash value designated in the policy table less any outstanding loans.
   (D) An amount equal to the net premiums paid less any outstanding loans.

5. Which of the following nonforfeiture options might Mr. Z select that would eliminate his right to reinstate his policy?

   (A) Cash
   (B) Reduced Paid-Up
   (C) Extended Term
   (D) None of the nonforfeiture options would eliminate his right to reinstate

6. If Mr. Z selects the Reduced Paid-Up nonforfeiture option, his coverage will continue

   (A) Until death or age 100, whichever occurs first, in the amount of $100,000.
   (B) Until death or age 100, whichever occurs first, in an amount stated in the policy's Table of Guaranteed Values.
   (C) For the length of time stated in the policy's Table of Guaranteed Values in the amount of $100,000.
   (D) For the length of time and in the amount stated in the policy's Table of Guaranteed Values.

7. The settlement option that offers the beneficiary the highest degree of flexibility is

   (A) Cash
   (B) Interest
   (C) Fixed Amount
   (D) Life Income Annuity

8. Assume that Joe dies leaving Jolene as the beneficiary of a $100,000 Term policy. Also assume that Joe did not select a settlement option prior to his death. Jolene may now select any of the following settlement options found in Joe's policy EXCEPT to have the proceeds

    (A) Invested in the stock market with the company acting as the money manager.
    (B) Left on deposit with the insurance company which will pay Jolene interest on the money.
    (C) Paid as a monthly income to Jolene in either a fixed amount or for a fixed number of years.
    (D) Paid to Jolene as a life income, with or without certain guarantees as available in the policy.

9. Which dividend option would result in the insured incurring a current year tax obligation?

    (A) Accumulate at Interest
    (B) Paid-up Life
    (C) Paid-up Additions
    (D) One Year Term

10. The nonforfeiture option that provides the same face amount of coverage as the original policy but for a lesser period of time is called:

    (A) Reduced Paid-Up
    (B) Paid-up Life
    (C) Extended Term
    (D) Re-entry Term

11. Installment payments of principal and interest for a fixed period of time are known as a(n)

    (A) Life Only Annuity
    (B) Straight (Pure) Life Annuity
    (C) Annuity Certain
    (D) Refund Life Annuity

CHAPTER 6 • LIFE POLICY OPTIONS QUIZ

12.   Which of the following settlement options guarantees at least the return of the original purchase price?

(A)   Straight Life Annuity
(B)   Installment Refund Life Annuity
(C)   Life Annuity with Period Certain
(D)   Joint and 2/3 Survivorship Life Annuity

END

QUIZ ANSWERS & EXPLANATIONS ON NEXT PAGE

© 2017 Pathfinder Corporation

CHAPTER 6
LIFE POLICY OPTIONS QUIZ ANSWER KEY

1. C. Dividends are not taxable, but interest earned on dividends would be taxed in the year in which it is earned.

2. D. Dividends are never guaranteed.

3. C. Extended Term insurance is the automatic option.

4. C. If Mr. Z surrenders the policy he would receive the cash value of his policy. However, if he had taken a policy loan and had not repaid it, that amount would be subtracted from the cash value.

5. A. If Mr. Z selects the cash option he has no right to reinstate his contract.

6. B. If Mr. Z selects the Reduced Paid-Up option it means his coverage period will remain the same (death or age 100), but the face amount of his policy will be reduced.

7. B. The Interest option is considered the most flexible of all of the settlement options.

8. A. Settlement options include: cash, interest option, fixed period or fixed amount annuity certain, and life annuity. There is no option that would have the insurance company acting as a stockbroker.

9. A. Dividends are not taxable, but interest earned on dividends would be taxed in the year in which it is earned.

10. C. The Extended Term nonforfeiture option means the face amount of the policy remains the same, but the coverage period is reduced.

11. C. An Annuity Certain pays out money in fixed amounts or over a fixed period of time until all funds have been paid. It is not a Life Annuity.

12. B. A Refund Life Annuity (both Installment Refund and Cash Refund) guarantees that if the annuitant dies before receiving an amount equal to the principal invested, the remaining balance will be paid to a beneficiary.

© 2017 Pathfinder Corporation

CHAPTER 7
SPECIALIZED LIFE INSURANCE
POLICIES & RIDERS

1. Which of the following life insurance policy riders does NOT require additional premium?

   (A)   Return of premium
   (B)   Cost of living
   (C)   Automatic premium loan
   (D)   Guaranteed insurability

2. Which of the following triggers an Automatic Premium Loan if this option is elected on the application of a Whole Life Policy?

   (A)   Failure to elect a nonforfeiture option on the application.
   (B)   Failure to reinstate the policy by the end of the reinstatement period.
   (C)   The election of a nonforfeiture value during the lifetime of the policy.
   (D)   Nonpayment of the premium at the end of the grace period.

3. A policyowner owns a life insurance policy and becomes permanently and totally disabled. Under the Waiver of Premium provision, she will receive which of the following benefits?

   (A)   Immediate payment of the face amount of the policy.
   (B)   The right to purchase additional insurance without submitting proof of insurability.
   (C)   The cash value in the policy plus the gross premiums paid.
   (D)   The premium will be waived throughout the length of the disability and her benefits will not be reduced in any way.

4. A typical Guaranteed Insurability option allows the policyowner/insured to purchase which of the following?

   (A)   Additional coverage on his own life providing he can show proof of insurability.
   (B)   A double indemnity rider in case of accidental death.
   (C)   Additional coverage on his own life without proof of insurability.
   (D)   Coverage on the life of his spouse, at specified intervals.

© 2017 Pathfinder Corporation

5. Which of the following statements concerning a Family (Protection) Policy is correct?

    (A) Individual policies are issued to cover each member of the family.
    (B) If the insured dies during a designated period as stated in the policy, the insurance company will pay an income to the surviving spouse for the remainder of that designated period.
    (C) The policy is terminated upon the death of the primary insured.
    (D) The policy covers the primary insured with Whole Life, and the spouse and children with Convertible Term.

6. Jolene is insured under a $100,000 face amount Whole Life Policy with a triple indemnity rider. If Jolene dies of a stroke while jogging, the insurance company will pay which of the following amounts?

    (A) $300,000
    (B) $200,000
    (C) $100,000
    (D) $0

7. All of the following statements about Modified Life and Graded Premium Whole Life policies are true EXCEPT:

    (A) The purpose for these contracts is to make protection less expensive in the early years of the contract.
    (B) Modified Life is simply Convertible Term, which converts to Whole Life.
    (C) The idea of Graded Premium is to charge a higher premium in the earlier years, followed by a lower premium in the later years.
    (D) Modified Life restricts the time in which the insured has to convert to Whole Life without proof of insurability.

8. Under a Family Policy, the nonforfeiture options may be utilized by

    (A) All family members insured under the policy.
    (B) The policyowner only.
    (C) The primary insured and his spouse only.
    (D) The beneficiary.

© 2017 Pathfinder Corporation

9. Joe Insured just purchased a $20,000 Juvenile Life policy on the life of his 10-year-old daughter, Betty Jo, and named himself as sole beneficiary. The policy has a Payor Benefit rider through age 21. If Joe dies five years from now, which of the following will occur?

    (A)   The insurance company will pay $20,000 to Joe's estate.
    (B)   The policy will lapse due to nonpayment of the premium.
    (C)   The Extended Term nonforfeiture option will automatically be triggered.
    (D)   Premiums on the policy will be waived until Betty Jo's 21st birthday.

10. Which of the following policies may be referred to as a last to die policy?

    (A)   Modified Life
    (B)   Joint Life
    (C)   Survivorship Life
    (D)   Joint and Survivorship Life Annuity

11. Which of the following statements is true regarding an Interest Sensitive Whole Life policy?

    (A)   Since the cash values are invested in the stock market, there is no guaranteed rate of return.
    (B)   The policy guarantees a minimum growth of cash value, but it may pay a higher rate of return based on current interest rates.
    (C)   The insurance company will pay a competitive rate of interest on the cash value, but there is no guaranteed minimum rate of return.
    (D)   Interest Sensitive Whole Life is the same as Variable Whole Life.

12. Which of the following is true concerning Accelerated Death Benefits?

    (A)   This provision allows the policyowner/insured to withdraw a portion of the face amount of the policy if he or she becomes terminally ill and is expected to die within a specified period such as six months or a year.
    (B)   This provision allows the insurance company to accelerate the policyowner's death.
    (C)   This provision allows the insured to borrow up to 100% of the cash value if the insured becomes terminally ill.
    (D)   This provision allows for the purchase of a Viatical Settlement.

© 2017 Pathfinder Corporation

13. Which of the following is NOT true about the Family (Protection) policy?

(A) Term riders can be added to a Whole Life policy to create a Family (Protection) policy.
(B) Children born after the issuance of the contract are covered without proof of insurability or increase in premium.
(C) Adopted children must show proof of insurability if they are to be covered.
(D) The Family (Protection) policy combines Whole Life and Convertible Term.

14. At age 40 Joe purchased a Re-Entry Term policy to age 65. If at age 45 Joe can establish insurability acceptable to the company, which of the following is true?

(A) He would be allowed to keep his Term policy with no change in rates.
(B) He could keep his Term policy with an increase in death benefit.
(C) He could keep his Term policy with a small decrease in premium rate.
(D) He will be permitted to convert his Term policy into a Whole Life policy.

15. Which of the following life insurance disability riders would be most appropriate for a Juvenile Life policy?

(A) Waiver of Premium
(B) Payor Benefit
(C) Disability Income
(D) Waiver of Cost of Insurance

16. An Equity indexed Life policy

(A) Is a Variable contract.
(B) Is tied to a Securities index like the S&P 500.
(C) Has its cash value invested in a separate account.
(D) Can only be sold by an agent who also holds a Securities license.

CHAPTER 7
SPECIALIZED LIFE INSURANCE POLICIES & RIDERS QUIZ

17.   The owner of a Modified Life policy should expect:

(A)   An increasing death benefit.
(B)   A decreasing death benefit.
(C)   An absence of cash value throughout the life of the policy.
(D)   An increasing premium.

18.   A life insurance policy with a Payor Benefit Rider protects:

(A)   The insurance company against misrepresentations should the insured become disabled.
(B)   The beneficiary by forbidding a change in beneficiary designations.
(C)   The insured from paying premiums until their 21st birthday if the policyowner becomes disabled.
(D)   The policyowner by providing income during any period of disability.

END

QUIZ ANSWERS & EXPLANATIONS ON NEXT PAGE

© 2017 Pathfinder Corporation

CHAPTER 7
SPECIALIZED LIFE INSURANCE
POLICIES & RIDERS QUIZ ANSWER KEY

1. C. The Automatic Premium Loan rider must be selected by the policyowner but it does not require additional premium.

2. D. If premium is not paid by the end of the grace period, the insurance company will execute a policy loan from the cash value of the policy and make the premium payment.

3. D. A Waiver of Premium rider states that if the policyowner is permanently and totally disabled, the premium on the policy will be waived, but that the policyowner's rights and benefits will not change in any way.

4. C. A Guaranteed Insurability rider permits the policyowner to buy additional amounts of insurance at selected dates or events without proof of insurability.

5. D. A Family Policy covers the policyowner with Whole Life insurance and the spouse and children with Convertible Term insurance.

6. C. A stroke is not an accident. Therefore, the policy would pay, but the rider would not.

7. C. The idea of both is to charge a lower premium in the early years of the contract, not a higher premium.

8. B. Only the policyowner has Whole Life insurance and would be the only insured with nonforfeiture benefits.

9. D. A Payor Benefit rider is used to insure a juvenile's policy will not lapse if the payor (the person who is paying the premiums) dies or becomes disabled.

10. C. Survivorship Life matures upon the death of the second insured, and thus could be called a last to die policy.

11. B. The company guarantees a minimum interest rate, but if they make more, so does the policyowner. If the company earns a higher rate of interest than projected, they will pay a higher rate of interest on the cash value.

© 2017 Pathfinder Corporation

12. A. Accelerated Death Benefits allow a portion of the face amount of the contract to be paid (up to 50%) if a certain trigger event occurs (such as terminal illness, need for an organ transplant etc.) Answer B is not correct. Typically, a company would only seek to accelerate the death of a policyowner if the policyowner were particularly annoying.

13. C. Both children born to, and children adopted by the family are automatically covered with no additional premium and no need to prove insurability.

14. C. Re-entry Term insurance means the insured will prove acceptable insurability at specified dates. If they are able to do so, premiums will decrease. If not, premiums will simply continue to increase at a normal rate.

15. B. A Payor Benefit rider is used to insure a juvenile's policy will not lapse if the payor (the person who is paying the premiums) dies or becomes disabled.

16. B. Equity Indexed products are always tied to an index like the Standard and Poor's 500.

17. D. Premiums are lower in the early years of the contract, but will gradually increase.

18. C. A Payor Benefit rider is used to insure a juvenile's policy will not lapse if the payor (the person who is paying the premiums) dies or becomes disabled.

CHAPTERS 8 & 9
BUSINESS & RETIREMENT USES
FLEXIBLE FEATURE POLICIES

1. Of the following, which is the most appropriate way to fund a Buy and Sell Agreement?

    (A) Joint Life
    (B) Survivorship Life
    (C) Split-Dollar
    (D) Decreasing Term

2. All of the following statements about a Keogh (HR-10) retirement plan are true EXCEPT

    (A) The plan must cover all full-time employees over age 21 who have one or more years of service.
    (B) Withdrawals from the plan prior to age 59 1/2 are subject to penalties.
    (C) Withdrawals from the plan must begin at age 70 1/2 in order to avoid late withdrawal penalties.
    (D) Annual contributions to the plan by the employer are unlimited in dollar amount.

3. A qualified participant in an Individual Retirement Account (IRA) may make tax-deductible contributions through all of the following investment vehicles EXCEPT an individual

    (A) Retirement account at a bank or savings and loan association.
    (B) Flexible premium retirement annuity issued by a life insurance company.
    (C) Universal Life insurance policy.
    (D) Retirement bond purchased from the United States government.

4. Dr. Davis is self-employed and has a Keogh plan in which he puts aside 8% of his income each year for retirement. Harriet Nelson has worked full time for Dr. Davis for one year and is 30 years old. Dr. Davis is required to do which of the following concerning Harriet's retirement?

    (A) He is not legally required to do anything.
    (B) He must contribute an amount equal to 4% of her salary to her retirement fund and she must match this amount.
    (C) He must withhold 8% of her salary to fund her Keogh plan.
    (D) He must put aside an amount equal to 8% of her salary from the earnings of his practice.

5. A 501C, not-for-profit, corporation would be eligible for which retirement plan?

    (A) Roth IRA
    (B) Keogh
    (C) 403 B/TSA
    (D) SEP

6. Harry and David are partners in a restaurant business. They establish a Buy and Sell Agreement funded by Term insurance under a Stock Redemption plan. Which of the following best describes the tax consequences of this agreement to the partnership?

    (A) The premiums are tax deductible and any death benefits are not subject to federal income tax.
    (B) The premiums are not tax deductible and any death benefits are subject to federal income tax.
    (C) The premiums are tax deductible but any death benefits are subject to federal income tax.
    (D) The premiums are not tax deductible but any death benefits are not subject to federal income tax.

Questions 7 - 11:

Choose from the contracts listed the one that is best described by the following. A contract may be used once, more than once or not at all.

    (A) Adjustable Life
    (B) Variable Whole Life
    (C) Universal Life
    (D) Variable Universal Life

© 2017 Pathfinder Corporation

CHAPTERS 8 & 9
BUSINESS & RETIREMENT USES / FLEXIBLE FEATURE POLICIES QUIZ

7. The policy type which has a guaranteed fixed minimum death benefit and a fixed premium, but the actual death benefit can increase according to the rate of return earned in the separate account.

    (A)   (B)   (C)   (D)

8. The policy type which always offers the protection element of the policy in the form of Term insurance, and there is a guaranteed minimum rate of return on the invested cash value.

    (A)   (B)   (C)   (D)

9. The policy type in which the policyowner may change the death benefit (within certain limits) according to his/her current needs, and the company invests the cash value of the policy in accordance with the directions of the policyowner in the separate account.

    (A)   (B)   (C)   (D)

10. The policy type which may be Term or Whole Life insurance and can easily be changed from one to the other.

    (A)   (B)   (C)   (D)

11. The policy type with a very flexible premium payment plan which is also a securities product and therefore requires that the producer also be licensed by the NASD or SEC.

    (A)   (B)   (C)   (D)

12. Maria owns an Adjustable Life policy. Maria could adjust any of the following EXCEPT

    (A)   The face amount
    (B)   The premium amount
    (C)   The type of plan (Term or Permanent Insurance)
    (D)   Where the cash value is invested

© 2017 Pathfinder Corporation

13. A client purchased a Universal Life policy from you several years ago. Which of the following actions can your client take?

(A) Add a second insured.
(B) Withdraw a portion of her cash value without interest or any obligation to repay (partial surrender).
(C) Substantially increase the face amount without proof of insurability.
(D) Change the investment vehicle for the policy's cash value.

14. The cash value of Hugh's Variable Universal Life policy is growing at the rate of 15%. In order to avoid placing Hugh in an unfavorable tax position, most insurers would likely

(A) Use Hugh's excess cash value to buy another policy.
(B) Reinvest Hugh's cash value at a lower rate.
(C) Raise the death benefit of Hugh's policy.
(D) Notify Hugh to stop paying his premiums.

15. Which of the following products would have a guaranteed minimum death benefit, a cash value that increases or decreases depending upon investment results, and nonforfeiture benefits?

(A) Universal Life
(B) Variable Whole Life
(C) Modified Life
(D) Adjustable Life

16. You own an IRA. What percent is vested?

(A) 100%
(B) 75%
(C) 50%
(D) 0%

17. Which of the following is NOT an example of third-party ownership?

(A) Key Employee Life Insurance
(B) Buy & Sell Life Insurance
(C) Group Life
(D) IRA accounts

© 2017 Pathfinder Corporation

18.   A nonqualified retirement plan is one which

(A)   Is designed for the exclusive benefit of the employees or their beneficiaries.

(B)   Must not discriminate in favor of officers, stockholders, or highly compensated employees.

(C)   Is formalized in writing and must be communicated to the employees in writing.

(D)   Does not qualify for special IRS tax treatment and therefore does allow for discrimination in favor of key officers, stockholders, or highly compensated employees.

19.   A cash withdrawal made from the cash value of a Universal Life Policy

(A)   Is normally free from taxes and penalties.

(B)   Is subject to tax and a penalty if the policyowner is not yet 59 1/2.

(C)   Must be repaid within one calendar year.

(D)   Must be rolled over into another policy in order to avoid taxes.

20.   In order to avoid taxation and a penalty, the proceeds from a qualified retirement plan that has been discontinued must be deposited into a Rollover IRA within how many days?

(A)   15 days.

(B)   30 days.

(C)   60 days.

(D)   120 days.

21.   A qualified pension plan has the following characteristics:

- The contributions can continue beyond age 70 1/2.
- The contributions are never tax deductible
- Qualified distributions of both principal and interest are exempt from income taxes.

The above described plan is a

(A)   SEP

(B)   TSA

(C)   IRA

(D)   Roth IRA

© 2017 Pathfinder Corporation

22. In a Variable Life contract, dollars are invested in:

(A) The general account.
(B) A reinsurance company.
(C) A separate account.
(D) An IRA.

23. Which of the following statements is true of the Old Age Survivors and Disability Insurance Program (OASDI: better known as Social Security)?

(A) In order to be fully insured under the program you have at least forty years of employment.
(B) The amount that you will receive as a Social Security retirement benefit will be dependent upon your Primary Insurance Amount (PIA).
(C) The definition of disability under Social Security is easier to qualify for than is normal under individual disability income policies.
(D) Most benefits only require that you are currently insured.

24. Which of the following is an eligibility requirement for Social Security Disability Income (SSDI) benefits?

(A) 5 months of disability
(B) Being at least age 50
(C) Being eligible for Medicaid
(D) Fully insured status

25. Which of the following is NOT true about Social Security (OASDI) benefit programs?

(A) Most benefits are payable if you are currently insured.
(B) Certain government employees, policemen with their own retirement system, and individuals covered by the Railroad Retirement Act, are not covered by Social Security.
(C) If you are qualified, your benefits are based on your Primary Insurance Amount (PIA).
(D) Benefits include retirement benefits, survivor benefits, and disability benefits.

26. Assume that you are seriously disabled and are eligible for Social Security Disability Income benefits. Your income benefits will be determined by which of the following?

   (A) The length of time that you have been disabled.
   (B) The type of coverages that your employer purchased under the Social Security Act.
   (C) Your age and current income at the time of your loss.
   (D) Your PIA, which is based upon your average monthly wage during your earning years.

27. Which of the following is NOT true in calculating your PIA?

   (A) Income earned above the Social Security limit is not counted in calculating your PIA.
   (B) You may eliminate your five lowest earning years in the PIA calculations.
   (C) You may eliminate any years during which you were disabled from your calculations.
   (D) Your unearned income will be included in your PIA calculations.

END

QUIZ ANSWERS & EXPLANATIONS ON NEXT PAGE

CHAPTERS 8 & 9
BUSINESS & RETIREMENT USES
FLEXIBLE FEATURE POLICIES
QUIZ ANSWER KEY

1. A. A Joint Life policy covers two lives and matures upon the death of the first.

2. D. Contributions to any qualified retirement plan are always limited by law. For a Keogh plan the annual contribution limit is the lesser of $40,000 or 100% of earned income.

3. C. As a general rule, life insurance cannot be used to fund a qualified retirement plan.

4. D. An employer with a Keogh plan must make a matching contribution (the same percentage) for any employee who has been with the company for more than a year, is over the age of 21, and who works more than 1000 hours a year.

5. C. A 403B Tax Sheltered Annuity is a qualified retirement plan established for use by 501C not-for-profit organizations.

6. D. The premiums are not tax deductible because the policy benefits the owners of the company. The death benefit from a life insurance policy is not subject to federal income tax.

7. B. Of the four choices, only Variable Whole Life has a fixed premium and a fixed, guaranteed minimum death benefit.

8. C. Only Universal and Variable Universal always offer the protection element of Term insurance. And only Universal would guarantee a minimum rate of return on invested cash value.

9. D. Separate investment accounts are only found in variable contracts. But because the policy mentioned in this question gives the policyowner the right to change the death benefit it means the death benefit is flexible, and thus Variable Universal Life is the correct answer.

10. A. Adjustable Life can be Term or Whole Life Insurance, and the policyowner has the right to change the type of protection from one to the other.

© 2017 Pathfinder Corporation

CHAPTERS 8 & 9
BUSINESS & RETIREMENT USES / FLEXIBLE FEATURE POLICIES
QUIZ ANSWER KEY

11.　D.　A securities product means it is a variable contract. The only variable contract that offers flexible premiums is Variable Universal Life.

12.　D.　An Adjustable Life policy does not allow the policyowner to control investment of the cash value.

13.　B.　A Universal Life policy would permit the policyowner to withdraw a portion of the cash value. Normally this withdrawal (partial surrender) can be made without interest, taxes or any obligation to repay.

14.　C.　Raising the death benefit would preclude his cash value growing faster than a Seven-Pay premium plan would for the new death benefit. This keeps the policy from being declared an MEC.

15.　B.　Variable Whole Life has a fixed premium and a fixed, guaranteed minimum death benefit. The cash value is invested in a separate account and is invested in accordance with the wishes of the policyowner.

16.　A.　If you own the IRA, all of the money invested is your money, which means you are 100% vested immediately.

17.　D.　Only you can own your IRA. A third party cannot own it.

18.　D.　Non-qualified means the plans do not qualify for special IRS tax treatment, and therefore can discriminate in favor of highly-paid employees. Qualified plans may not discriminate.

19.　A.　A Universal Life policy would permit the policyowner to withdraw a portion of the cash value. Normally this withdrawal (partial surrender) can be made without interest, taxes or any obligation to repay.

20.　C.　By law, proceeds must be rolled over into the IRA within 60 days. Failure to do so would result in taxes and a 10% penalty.

21.　D.　Roth IRA contributions are never tax deductible, but when the money is paid out at retirement, neither the premiums paid nor the interest earned is taxable.

22.　C.　Separate investment accounts are always found in variable contracts.

© 2017 Pathfinder Corporation

CHAPTERS 8 & 9
BUSINESS & RETIREMENT USES / FLEXIBLE FEATURE POLICIES
QUIZ ANSWER KEY

23. B. Your Primary Insurance Amount will determine the benefit you receive. The PIA is based upon your average monthly wage during the years you were employed.

24. D. Fully Insured Status means that you are entitled to all benefits offered by Social Security. To be considered fully insured, you must have paid into Social Security for at least forty quarters.

25. A. Currently insured individuals only have survivor benefits. Fully insured individuals are entitled to all benefits.

26. D. Your Primary Insurance Amount will determine the benefit you receive. The PIA is based upon your average monthly wage during the years you were employed.

27. D. PIA calculations only consider earned income.

© 2017 Pathfinder Corporation

CHAPTER 10
HEALTH INSURANCE FUNDAMENTALS

1. Which of the following terms refers to a policy provision that eliminates coverage for a specific risk?

    (A) Omission
    (B) Exclusion
    (C) Limitation
    (D) Deletion

2. Which of the following is the most restrictive A&H renewal provision for the insured?

    (A) Conditionally Renewable
    (B) Optionally Renewable
    (C) Guaranteed Renewable
    (D) Noncancellable

3. Which of the following statements is true about the Probationary Period provision in a Health Insurance Contract?

    (A) It is a permanent exclusion.
    (B) It applies to every claim.
    (C) It begins on the policy's effective date.
    (D) It is coordinated with the Elimination (Waiting) Period.

4. One of the primary reasons for using deductibles in health policies is to reduce

    (A) Adverse selection.
    (B) The need for certain exclusions.
    (C) Over-utilization of the policies.
    (D) The number of covered conditions.

© 2017 Pathfinder Corporation

5.   Which of the following would NOT be consistent with the term Managed Care?

(A)   Controlled access to health care providers, such as doctors.
(B)   Utilization review, which is a method of assuring that patients are not given an excess level of medical care.
(C)   Preventive care which is designed to minimize the overall cost of health care.
(D)   Fee for service arrangements which allow the patient to visit any doctor that he or she wishes.

6.   A Guaranteed Renewable A&H Policy permits the insurance company to do which of the following?

(A)   Change policy provisions at specified times in order for the issuing company to remain profitable.
(B)   Change premium rates under certain conditions at renewal.
(C)   Require new proof of insurability at renewal.
(D)   Lengthen the Elimination Period under certain conditions.

7.   A Health Policy which guarantees the premium and coverages through age 65 would be referred to as

(A)   Optionally Renewable
(B)   Conditionally Renewable
(C)   Noncancellable
(D)   Guaranteed Renewable

8.   A Conditionally Renewable A&H Policy gives the insurance company which of the following rights?

(A)   The right to decline renewal because of a change in the insured's health.
(B)   The right to decline renewal if the insured changes to a more hazardous occupation.
(C)   The right to lengthen the Probationary Period under certain conditions.
(D)   The right to cancel the coverage if the insured becomes disabled.

9. An individual may have one major problem that causes them to be uninsurable. The name of the rider that could exclude coverage for this specific condition is referred to as which of the following?

    (A) Ghost rider
    (B) Impairment rider
    (C) COLA rider
    (D) Waiver of Premium rider

10. Which of the following statements about the Free Look provision in an A&H Policy is true?

    (A) It assures the applicant of a refund of premium for a limited period of time.
    (B) The Free Look period begins on the date of application.
    (C) The Free Look period begins on the policy effective date.
    (D) The Free Look period for most contracts is 90 days.

11. Al owns an individual Major Medical policy. Which of the following statements is true about injuries Al sustains during the policy while on active duty in the armed services?

    (A) They are covered after a 2-year waiting period.
    (B) They are covered immediately on the policy date.
    (C) They are covered if the insured is a member of a United Nations force.
    (D) They are excluded from coverage.

12. All of the following statements are true about the taxation of disability income and medical expense benefits EXCEPT

    (A) Disability income benefits received from a policy that you individually own are not taxed.
    (B) Disability income benefits that you receive from a disability income program provided by your employer are taxed as ordinary income.
    (C) Regardless of who owns the policy, medical expense benefits that you receive are not taxed as ordinary income.
    (D) The premium paid by an employer for group disability income or group medical expense coverage is not deductible as a business expense.

© 2017 Pathfinder Corporation

13. Health care coverages are being provided by all of the following EXCEPT

   (A)   POS Plans
   (B)   PPOs
   (C)   HMOs
   (D)   TPAs

14. Health insurance policies include the pre-existing conditions exclusion in order to protect the insurance company against

   (A)   Malingering
   (B)   Overinsurance
   (C)   Overutilization
   (D)   Adverse selection

15. The provision in an A&H policy which states that insurance is provided in exchange for the representations in the application and payment of the premium is found in the

   (A)   Benefit Provision
   (B)   Consideration clause
   (C)   K.A.T. Clause
   (D)   Preexisting Conditions clause

For questions 16-18:

Choose the health plan below which best fits the description given. Each plan may be used once, more than once, or not at all.

   (A)   Blue Cross/Blue Shield service organizations
   (B)   Health Maintenance Organization (HMO)
   (C)   Point of Service (POS) Plans
   (D)   Preferred Provider Organization (PPO)

16. A health care system designed to function within the boundaries of a specific community under which the organization typically owns the clinics and perhaps even a hospital and which encourages preventive care.

   (A)   (B)   (C)   (D)

© 2017 Pathfinder Corporation

17. This plan allows the insured employee to choose the most appropriate health plan whenever a medical loss occurs.

(A)   (B)   (C)   (D)

18. A plan in which an insured receives financial incentives for seeking services from a list of medical providers.

(A)   (B)   (C)   (D)

19. Which of the following is true regarding occupational injury or illness?

(A) Medical Expense policies are the primary coverage for occupational injuries and Workers Compensation is the excess coverage.
(B) Disability Income policies are the primary coverage for occupational injuries and Workers Compensation is the excess coverage.
(C) Medical Expense policies exclude occupational injuries.
(D) Disability Income policies never cover occupational injuries.

20. When an HMO pays its providers a flat dollar sum per HMO member, the process is called

(A) Capitation
(B) Restitution
(C) Decapitation
(D) Incapacitation

21. In a typical Point of Service (POS) Plan if an insured uses an outside provider, it will result in

(A) The insured being denied coverage.
(B) The insured paying a higher co-insurance charge.
(C) The insured being billed to reimburse the insurer for any payments made.
(D) The insured's policy being cancelled.

CHAPTER 10 • HEALTH INSURANCE FUNDAMENTALS QUIZ

22. The term "ambulatory" care refers to which of the following?

    (A)   Outpatient treatment at a hospital or doctor's office.
    (B)   Inpatient treatment at a hospital or doctor's office.
    (C)   Rehabilitation for patients who cannot walk unassisted.
    (D)   Rehabilitation for patients who can walk without assistance.

23. Cost containment in health care delivery is promoted by all the following EXCEPT

    (A)   Gatekeeper
    (B)   Fee-for-service care
    (C)   Preventive care
    (D)   Outpatient care

24. All of the following are true concerning a Health Savings Account (HSA) EXCEPT

    (A)   The savings account portion is designed to pay for low cost medical procedures like doctor visits.
    (B)   Catastrophic medical expense costs are covered by the Major Medical portion of the coverage.
    (C)   Deposits remaining in the HSA may be totally withdrawn after age 59 1/2 without taxes or penalty.
    (D)   Total withdrawals for non-medical purposes from the HSA after age 65 trigger a tax liability on both the contributions and interest earned.

END

QUIZ ANSWERS & EXPLANATIONS ON NEXT PAGE

CHAPTER 10
HEALTH INSURANCE FUNDAMENTALS
QUIZ ANSWER KEY

1. B. Exclusions eliminate coverage.

2. B. Optionally Renewable is the most restrictive because the insurance company makes the decision on whether or not the contract will be renewed.

3. C. Probationary Periods begin on the policy's effective date. There will be no coverage for an illness that happens during the Probationary Period.

4. C. Deductibles discourage insureds from seeking medical care for minor problems.

5. D. Managed Care is a term related to efforts by a Health Insurance company to control costs. Allowing an insured to seek care on demand from any source would contribute to higher costs.

6. B. Premiums will increase at renewability. Increases can be due to age of insured and rising costs of medical care, but health of the insured will not be a factor.

7. C. Noncancellable means a guaranteed right to renew at a guaranteed price.

8. B. Conditionally means a right to renew unless the insured retires early or changes to a more hazardous occupation.

9. B. Impairment Rider is also known as an Exclusion Rider.

10. A. The Free Look period begins on the date the policy is delivered and it assures the applicant of a refund of premium for a limited time.

11. D. Losses incurred while on active military duty are always excluded.

12. D. Medical Expense benefits are never taxed. Disability Income benefits would be taxed if your employer paid the premium. The employer will always be able to deduct premium for either medical expense or group disability income policies.

© 2017 Pathfinder Corporation

CHAPTER 10 • HEALTH INSURANCE FUNDAMENTALS
QUIZ ANSWER KEY

13.   D.   A TPA (Third Party Administrator) administers a self-funded plan; it does not provide health care coverage.

14.   D.   Adverse selection is the tendency for sick people to apply for insurance before healthy people do. By temporarily excluding pre-existing conditions, the company won't get stuck with a bad risk that would require an immediate payout of benefits.

15.   B.   Premium money and the application represent the insured's consideration and would be found in the Consideration Clause.

16.   B.   Only HMOs own clinics.

17.   C.   Point of Service lets the employee decide which plan to use when they need the service.

18.   D.   PPOs offer a list of providers.

19.   C.   Medical Expense policies exclude occupational losses because they are better covered by Worker's Comp.

20.   A.   Capitation. No other answer here makes sense.

21.   B.   The insured pays more out of their own pocket for the right to choose to go outside the HMO.

22.   A.   Ambulatory equals outpatient.

23.   B.   Fee-for-service allows the insured to choose any medical provider and thus would not contain costs.

24.   C.   Money in a Health Savings Account can be removed without penalty at age 65, not 59½. However, if you remove the money for non-medical reasons, you would owe taxes on the contributions and the interest earned.

CHAPTER 11
DISABILITY INCOME

1. All of the following statements about partial disability are true EXCEPT

    (A) The benefit amount for a partial disability is usually the same as that for total disability.
    (B) The definition of partial disability is the inability to perform one or more important duties of an insured's regular occupation.
    (C) A partial disability must follow a period of total disability.
    (D) Partial Disability benefits encourage a person to return to work on a limited basis during a convalescent period.

2. Al owned a Disability Income policy providing a 10-year accident and 10-year sickness insurance benefit period. The policy had a 7-day Elimination Period and a 30-day Probationary Period provision. If Al was hospitalized for an illness 9 days after the effective date of the policy, the maximum coverage immediately available would be which of the following?

    (A) 20 years of sickness benefits
    (B) 10 years of sickness benefits
    (C) 21 days of sickness benefits
    (D) None

3. Disability income policies generally have a benefit limit. This benefit limit is usually set as a percentage of which of the following amounts?

    (A) Gross income before tax.
    (B) Earned income plus unearned income before tax.
    (C) Earned income.
    (D) Earned income plus unearned income after tax.

4. Which of the following statements about the Waiver of Premium provision in an individual Disability Income policy is true?

    (A) Under this provision no premium is required from the onset of the disability.
    (B) The insured must be totally disabled.
    (C) The insured must be permanently disabled.
    (D) This benefit is only available as a rider.

© 2017 Pathfinder Corporation

CHAPTER 11 • DISABILITY INCOME QUIZ

5. You own a Disability Income policy that pays $600 per week. Which of the following is true concerning the taxation of your Disability Income benefits?

(A) Any benefits will be fully taxable as ordinary income.
(B) None of your disability income benefits will be taxable.
(C) Disability income benefits are taxable only to the extent that they replace your normal income.
(D) Disability income benefits are taxable only to the extent that they exceed the $600 weekly exclusion.

6. You own a Business Overhead Expense policy for your business and you are disabled for five months. The policy would pay benefits towards all of your following expenses EXCEPT:

(A) The office rent
(B) The salaries of your employees
(C) The business utility bills
(D) Your own lost income

7. A Guaranteed Insurability (Future Income) provision in an A&H policy states which of the following?

(A) The insured's contract may not be cancelled at the option of the insurance company.
(B) The insured can buy additional amounts of monthly Disability Income insurance on specified dates in the future without proof of insurability.
(C) Income benefit limits will automatically be increased each year at the rate of inflation.
(D) Benefit limits will be coordinated and adjusted based upon the disabled person's ability to earn future income.

8.   Helen is an insurance salesperson whose job is defined as calling on customers in their homes. She is covered by her own Disability Income insurance plan. Helen breaks her leg and although she can still go to the supermarket and take care of herself, she is unable to do her job for eight weeks. Under which definition of disability would Helen most probably be able to collect benefits for this loss?

(A)   Presumptive Total Disability
(B)   Any Occupation
(C)   Own Occupation
(D)   Hospital Confinement

9.   Nicole owns a long term Disability Income policy with a 30 day Elimination Period and a Recurrent Disability provision. Nicole is disabled for three months following a serious car accident. Shortly after she returns to work, she suffers a relapse and is disabled for an additional three months. Which of the following payments would be made under her Disability Income policy?

(A)   Nicole will receive a total of six months of disability income benefits.
(B)   Nicole will receive a total of five months of disability income benefits.
(C)   Nicole will receive a total of four months of disability income benefits.
(D)   Nicole will not receive any disability income benefits.

10.   Which of the following types of health policies would contain an elimination period?

(A)   Business Disability Buy-Sell
(B)   Blanket Medical Expense
(C)   Comprehensive Major Medical
(D)   Accidental Death and Dismemberment

11.   Which of the following is true of the residual disability benefit?

(A)   The residual disability benefit is the same as the recurrent disability benefit.
(B)   The residual disability benefit makes up for income that cannot be earned as a result of a permanent partial disability.
(C)   The residual disability benefit provides the insured with a shorter benefit period than the partial disability benefit provides.
(D)   The residual disability benefit normally pays 50% of the total disability benefit.

© 2017 Pathfinder Corporation

CHAPTER 11 • DISABILITY INCOME QUIZ

From the Disability Income policies below, choose the one that best fits the description given for questions 12 - 15. Each policy may be used once, more than once, or not at all.

(A) Individual Disability Income Protection
(B) Business Overhead Expense
(C) Key Employee/Person Disability Income
(D) Business Disability Buyout/Disability Buy-Sell

12. A policy under which benefits are payable to the insured's employer if the insured becomes disabled. The employer uses the benefit to pay for a temporary replacement for the disabled employee or, in many cases, as a salary continuation plan for the disabled employee.

    (A)   (B)   (C)   (D)

13. A coverage designed to provide benefits to a corporation to buy out a disabled stockholder/director's share of the business. The policy generally pays an installment benefit to the corporation for up to one year and then pays out a lump sum benefit.

    (A)   (B)   (C)   (D)

14. A policy which pays a substitute paycheck to the insured if he or she has an accident or suffers from an illness which satisfies the definition of disability in the contract.

    (A)   (B)   (C)   (D)

15. A policy which will pay the expenses of a business in the event that the person responsible for the earnings of the business becomes disabled (such as a doctor, lawyer, engineer or architect).

    (A)   (B)   (C)   (D)

© 2017 Pathfinder Corporation

16. The Elimination (Waiting) Period, which is often included in Disability Income Contracts, is the period

   (A) During which the insurance company makes benefit payments to the insured.
   (B) During which the policyowner must report a disability to the insurance company.
   (C) Between the policy issue date and the date benefit payments begin.
   (D) Between the onset of a disability and the date the insured becomes eligible for benefit payments.

17. All of the following are true about an elimination period and a probationary period as found in health policies EXCEPT

   (A) The elimination period starts on the date disability begins and is a deductible expressed in terms of time.
   (B) The probationary period is a period of time beginning with the policy effective date during which there is no coverage for illness.
   (C) An elimination period is only found in Disability Income policies.
   (D) An elimination period is designed to screen out pre-existing illnesses.

18. Key Employee Health policies

   (A) Are only issued by HMO's.
   (B) Are only issued by POS plans.
   (C) Have dependent coverages.
   (D) May be used to fund sick pay.

19. Presumptive Total Disability would pay in all following circumstances EXCEPT:

   (A) Loss of sight in one eye.
   (B) Loss of hearing.
   (C) Loss of the power of speech.
   (D) Loss of use of an arm and a leg.

END

QUIZ ANSWERS & EXPLANATIONS ON NEXT PAGE

© 2017 Pathfinder Corporation

CHAPTER 11
DISABILITY INCOME QUIZ ANSWER KEY

1. A. The benefit for partial disability would be less because the insured is working part time and earning income.

2. D. Illness that occurs during the Probationary Period is not covered.

3. C. Benefit limit is based solely on earned income.

4. B. Waiver of Premium is built-in to Disability Income policies and it requires the insured be totally disabled not permanently disabled.

5. B. Not taxed because you own the policy.

6. D. Business Overhead Expense policies pay for rent, utility bills, and employee salaries, but not for the lost income of the business owner.

7. B. Guaranteed Insurability means a chance to buy more insurance. Do not confuse with Guaranteed Renewability which means the right to renew a contract.

8. C. If she can't do her specific job and wants to receive benefits Own Occupation would be the definition she would want in her contract.

9. B. Two months for the original period of disability plus three more for the second occurrence. Recurrent disability provision states that if an insured returns to work after a covered disability and a relapse occurs within six months, benefits will be paid with no new Elimination Period.

10. A. Elimination Periods are only found in disability contracts. Of the four choices, only Business Disability Buy-Sell is a disability income policy.

11. B. Residual Disability addresses the problem of partial disability. It can pay a portion of the disability income benefit for as long as the partial disability lasts.

12. C. Key Employee Disability policies pay the employer.

13. D. Disability Buy-Sell policies are designed to buy out the interest of a disabled partner or owner.

© 2017 Pathfinder Corporation

14.   A.   This is the only answer that fits.

15.   B.   Business Overhead Expense policies keep the business operating during the period of time the person responsible for the earnings of the business is disabled.

16.   D.   Elimination Periods are time-based deductibles that start on the date the insured becomes disabled. Once the Elimination Period has been satisfied, the insured is eligible to receive benefits.

17.   D.   Probationary Periods screen out pre-existing conditions. Elimination Periods control over-utilization.

18.   D.   Key Employee Disability Income policies are not actually designed to fund employee sick pay but they can be used for that purpose.

19.   A.   Have to lose sight in both eyes.

CHAPTERS 12 - 14
MEDICAL EXPENSE, LTC, MSP & AD&D

1. Under the LTC and MSP marketing requirement regulations, which of the following questions would you NOT have to ask in the original fact finding interview?

    (A)   Are you covered by Medicaid?
    (B)   Do you intend to replace any of your present health care coverages with this policy?
    (C)   Do you have any other MSPs or LTC policies in force?
    (D)   How many children do you have?

2. Under an AD&D policy with a principal sum of $5,000 and a capital sum of $2,500, how much would the policyowner/insured receive for the loss of one eye?

    (A) $5,000
    (B) $2,500
    (C) $1,250
    (D) $0

3. The three types of benefits found in a typical Medical Expense policy are

    (A)   Hospital, Surgical, and Medical.
    (B)   Vision Care, Prescription Drug, and Dental.
    (C)   Hospital Indemnity, Blanket, and Disability Income.
    (D)   Dread Disease, Travel Accident, and AD&D.

4. The Coinsurance clause of a health insurance policy specifies that

    (A)   If the insured is covered simultaneously by two policies, then the two insurance companies involved will coordinate the benefits payable to the insured so that the insured does not make a profit.
    (B)   If two companies would pay on a claim, then the companies will split the claim payments equally.
    (C)   One insurance company may purchase reinsurance from another company to transfer some of the first company's risk to the second company.
    (D)   The insurance company covering the risk will only pay a percentage of the covered expenses.

© 2017 Pathfinder Corporation

5.   The purpose of the Coinsurance clause in Major Medical policies is to

(A)   Force the insured to pay the larger claims from personal resources.
(B)   Encourage the insured to satisfy the deductible.
(C)   Motivate the insured to minimize unnecessary care.
(D)   Encourage the insured to purchase an adequate amount of health insurance.

6.   B has a Major Medical policy with a deductible of $200, an 80/20 Coinsurance clause, a $10,000 Stop Loss, and a $1,000,000 lifetime benefit. If B has never submitted a prior claim under the policy and suffers a covered loss of $5,400, how much will the insurance company pay?

(A) $1,040
(B) $1,240
(C) $4,160
(D) $4,320

7.   A family medical expense policy generally must do all of the following EXCEPT:

(A)   Continue coverage beyond age 19 for handicapped dependents who are incapable of self-sustaining employment and chiefly dependent upon the policyowner for support and maintenance.
(B)   Automatically cover newborn children from the moment of birth as long as the policyowner notifies the insurance company within 31 days of the birth and pays additional premium if required.
(C)   Cover a newly adopted child from the date of placement.
(D)   Automatically cover the spouse of a dependent child.

8.   The minimum level of renewability that can be used when writing an LTC policy or MSP is which of the following?

(A)   Noncancellable
(B)   Guaranteed renewable
(C)   Conditionally renewable
(D)   Optionally renewable

© 2017 Pathfinder Corporation

9.   MSP regulations specify ten standard benefit plans, designated A through J. Which of the following is true about the marketing of these plans?

(A)   Every company that sells MSPs must offer Plan A.
(B)   Every company that markets MSPs must offer all ten plans.
(C)   At least five of the ten plans must be offered by any company marketing MSP plans.
(D)   Every company that sells MSPs must offer Plan J .

10.   All of the following are types of Major Medical deductibles EXCEPT:

(A)   Integrated
(B)   Corridor
(C)   Minor
(D)   Flat

11.   Which of the following policy types could pay a stated amount benefit for the loss of one eye?

(A)   MSP
(B)   LTC
(C)   AD&D
(D)   ETC

12.   An LTC policy may be cancelled because of

(A)   The death of the insured's spouse.
(B)   The deterioration of the insured's health.
(C)   A materially untrue statement on the application found within the contestable period.
(D)   The insured reaching the termination age.

13. Kate wishes to purchase a custodial/residential health care policy which will pay for nursing home type services such as getting in and out of bed, dressing, bathing, eating, etc. Which of the following policies would be most appropriate for you to recommend?

(A) Medicare Supplement
(B) Long-Term Care
(C) Variable Annuity
(D) Hospital Indemnity

14. Which of the following best describes the primary purpose of a Medicare Supplement policy?

(A) To provide medical expense coverage for people over age 65.
(B) To pay for medical expenses that Medicare will not pay for.
(C) To supplement the benefits available under Medicaid for those people who are eligible for both programs.
(D) To provide disability income benefits for those people receiving Medicare benefits.

Questions 15-17 refer to the following situation:

Frank Fritter is covered by a Medical Expense Plan with the following features: 80/20 percent coinsurance clause, $200 deductible, and a $1500 Base plan. He suffers a major illness, is hospitalized and incurs covered medical bills totaling $8700, plus a loss of income totaling $7000.

15. How much will the company pay under the coinsurance portion of the coverage?

(A) $ 5,600
(B) $ 6,800
(C) $ 7,100
(D) $12,600

16. How much will Frank's policy pay towards his lost income?

(A) $7,000
(B) $5,600
(C) It depends on his elimination period.
(D) Nothing

© 2017 Pathfinder Corporation

17.   What is the total amount that Frank's insurance company will pay on this claim?

    (A) $ 5,600
    (B) $ 7,100
    (C) $ 8,500
    (D) $14,100

18.   The procedure by which benefits of an A&H policy are transferred from the policyowner to the health care provider is known as

    (A)   Transfer of value
    (B)   Estoppel
    (C)   Buy/sell
    (D)   Assignment

19.   Which of the following policy types would provide for rights for dependent children?

    (A)   AD&D
    (B)   LTC
    (C)   MSP
    (D)   Major Medical

20.   Which of the following would NOT be considered a limited health care policy?

    (A)   Hospital Indemnity
    (B)   Major Medical
    (C)   Dread Disease
    (D)   Blanket

21.   Grandpa Joe, at age 85, can no longer dress, bathe, eat or take his medication without assistance. These limitations are considered to be which of the following?

    (A)   A sickness
    (B)   An accident
    (C)   A disability
    (D)   An activity of daily life

22.   Benefits provided by a Major Medical expense policy would NOT include

    (A)   Hospice benefits.
    (B)   Home health care.
    (C)   Custodial care.
    (D)   Hospital room and board expense.

23.   Grandpa Joe buys a Medicare Supplement policy on July 1. He had suffered a heart attack 12 months earlier. Any heart problems

    (A)   Are covered.
    (B)   Are excluded for 6 months.
    (C)   Are subject to an Impairment Rider.
    (D)   Are covered by Medicare, but are not covered by a Medicare Supplement policy.

24.   LTC policies are geared to provide benefits

    (A)   Only in licensed facilities.
    (B)   For acute care.
    (C)   In the least restrictive care environment.
    (D)   To supplement Disability Income policies.

25.   Medicaid can best be described as a program that

    (A)   Provides retirement benefits to those with at least 40 quarters of service.
    (B)   Is administered by the private sector of the commercial insurance industry.
    (C)   Provides financial aid to parents with dependent children.
    (D)   Provides medical benefits to those who are generally considered to be poor and one of the following: over age 65, blind or disabled.

26. Which of the following best describes Medicare?

    (A)   It is a social assistance program which provides medical expense benefits to the financially needy who qualify.

    (B)   It is a federal program which provides long-term custodial nursing home care to the elderly.

    (C)   It is a social insurance program which provides medical expense benefits to those who are eligible.

    (D)   It is a government insurance program which pays covered individuals and their eligible dependents lifetime monthly retirement benefits.

27. All of the following are characteristics of Medicare Part B (Supplementary Medical Insurance) EXCEPT

    (A)   It is a voluntary program.

    (B)   Its primary benefit is physicians and surgical services.

    (C)   It is issued by insurance companies.

    (D)   It requires payment of premium by the participant.

28. Which of the following is NOT true of Medicare Benefits?

    (A)   Medicare Part A would cover such benefits as a semi-private room and oxygen.

    (B)   Supplementary Medical Insurance (Part B) would pay for ambulance services.

    (C)   Medicare can pay for a stay in a skilled nursing facility but only directly following hospitalization.

    (D)   Supplementary Medical Insurance (Part B) eliminates the need for a Medicare Supplement Policy (MSP).

29. Which of the following statements is NOT true concerning Medicaid (Title 19)?

    (A)   Medicaid will pay for what Medicare will not pay for if you are entitled to both programs.

    (B)   Medicaid is an assistance program rather than an insurance program.

    (C)   All individuals can use Medicaid as a substitute for an LTC policy.

    (D)   Medicaid is administered by each state's Department of Public Welfare.

30.   Medicare is administered by

    (A)   Each state's Department of Public Welfare.
    (B)   Centers for Medicare and Medicaid Services.
    (C)   COBRA
    (D)   NASD

31.   The primary purpose of Medicaid is to

    (A)   Pay for expenses not covered by Medicare.
    (B)   Provide disability income benefits to people on Medicare.
    (C)   Provide medical expense coverage to the needy.
    (D)   Provide funds for people injured in natural disasters.

32.   Medicare Part B:

    (A)   Is required in order to receive Medicare Part A.
    (B)   Must be specifically requested.
    (C)   Is automatic unless declined.
    (D)   Is sold by private insurers.

33.   Medicare Part A benefits covering nursing home stays require all of the following EXCEPT

    (A)   Three days hospitalization before admission to the nursing home.
    (B)   Admission to the nursing home within 30 days of discharge from the hospital.
    (C)   The need for skilled nursing care.
    (D)   The need for assistance in performing the activities of daily living (ADLs).

END

QUIZ ANSWERS & EXPLANATIONS ON NEXT PAGE

CHAPTERS 12 -14
MEDICAL EXPENSE, LTC, MSP, & AD&D
QUIZ ANSWER KEY

1. D. These policies are not intended to support children.

2. B. Lose two parts- face amount paid. Lose one part- half the face amount.

3. A. The only logical answer. Remember the Base plans.

4. D. Coinsurance helps control over-utilization of the contract by requiring the insured to share costs with the insurance company.

5. C. See #4 above.

6. C. $5400 claim minus the $200 deductible paid by insured equals $5200. Of the $5200 the company pays 80%, or $4160.

7. D. The company is stuck with a handicapped child but not their marital partner.

8. B. MSPs and LTC Policies must have the highest levels of renewability. They can be no less than Guaranteed Renewable.

9. A. If you want to sell MSPs you must offer plan A.

10. C. There is no such thing as a minor deductible.

11. C. Accidental Death and Dismemberment. Hopefully you did not answer D. ETC stands for etcetera.

12. C. Lying on the application can lead to the benefits being contested.

13. B. Long-Term Care policies provided for custodial care.

14. B. Medicare Supplement policies supplement Medicare.

15. A. $8700 claim minus a $1500 base plan which is paid by the company equals $7200. Subtract the $200 deductible paid by Frank and the balance is $7000. Of the $7000 the company pays 80%, or $5600.

© 2017 Pathfinder Corporation

CHAPTERS 12 - 14
MEDICAL EXPENSE, LTC, MSP & AD&D QUIZ ANSWER KEY

16. D. This is a Medical Expense Policy, not a Disability Income Policy.

17. B. $5600 from co-insurance plus $1500 base plan equals $7100.

18. D. Assignment in Life insurance means assigning ownership. Assignment in Health Insurance means assigning benefits.

19. D. Only Medical Expense policies cover the entire family.

20. B. Major Medical is not a limited health policy.

21. D. Bathing, dressing etc. are Activities of Daily Living.

22. C. Custodial Care is better covered elsewhere a Long Term Care insurance policy.

23. A. In an MSP, law only permits the insurance company to look back six months to discover a pre-existing condition. Since Joe's heart attack occurred 12 months before he bought the policy, it would not be considered a pre-existing condition.

24. C LTC Policies provide care in the least restrictive alternative possible.

25. D. Broke plus one.

26. C. Medicare is insurance - not assistance. It provides medical expense coverage, not custodial care and not retirement benefits.

27. C. Parts A and B of Medicare are purchased through the government.

28. D. With parts A and B of Medicare, there is still a need for an MSP.

29. C. If you are broke plus one and eligible for Medicaid you would not need LTC. Hopefully our entire population of retirees is not broke.

30. B. By definition.

31. C. Aid equals Welfare.

32. C. Sort of optional... automatic unless declined.

33. D. Medicare is not a substitute for LTC.

© 2017 Pathfinder Corporation

CHAPTER 15
UNIFORM INDIVIDUAL HEALTH
POLICY PROVISIONS

1.   Burt, a full-time insurance producer, purchases a $1500 per month Disability Income policy to protect his income. A year later, he inherits a farm and changes his occupation to farmer. However, he failed to notify his insurance company, Turpitude Mutual, of his change to a higher risk occupation. Shortly thereafter he is injured in a farming accident and disabled for eight months. The company will probably

   (A)   Deny the claim on the basis of misrepresentation.
   (B)   Pay $1500 per month but demand that Burt make back payment of additional premiums for the entire period during which he was a farmer.
   (C)   Pay $1500 per month.
   (D)   Pay somewhat less than $1500 per month.

2.   The required provision which states that the insurance company must pay to a named beneficiary if one exists is called

   (A)   Proof of Loss
   (B)   Payment of Claims
   (C)   Change of Beneficiary
   (D)   Time of Payment of Claims

3.   Can an insurance company require an autopsy of a deceased insured under the Uniform Policy Provisions Law?

   (A)   Yes, under all circumstances.
   (B)   No, at no time can this be required.
   (C)   Yes, where it is not prohibited by state law.
   (D)   No, except where special permission is granted by the deceased's spouse or family.

© 2017 Pathfinder Corporation

4.   The Grace Period provision provides for all of the following EXCEPT a grace period of

(A)   7 days for a weekly premium policy.
(B)   10 days for a monthly premium policy.
(C)   30 days for a quarterly premium policy.
(D)   31 days for an annual premium policy.

5.   Bunco Joe is continuing his life of crime. While running away from the scene of a robbery he has just committed, Bunco suffers a heart attack and ends up in the hospital. However, he is covered by a Major Medical Expense insurance from Mutual of Purgatory and submits a claim for his loss. The company will probably

(A)   Pay the claim as a heart attack is a covered loss.
(B)   Refuse to pay the claim because it would be covered under Workers Compensation.
(C)   Deny the claim because Bunco is a habitual offender.
(D)   Deny the claim because Bunco was involved in an illegal occupation when he suffered the heart attack.

6.   Which of the following statements about the optional Change of Occupation provision in a Disability Income policy is true?

(A)   It allows the insurance company to deny benefits if the insured changes his occupation without notifying the insurance company.
(B)   It establishes the formula by which adjustments are made in policy premiums in the event the insured changes to a more hazardous occupation.
(C)   It voids the policy if the insured suffers an otherwise compensable loss while engaged in an illegal occupation.
(D)   It sets forth the rights and obligations of the insurance company and the insured in the event the insured engages in a more hazardous or less hazardous occupation.

7. Which of the following is NOT true of the A&H Reinstatement provision?

(A) As long as the policyowner submits proof of insurability and all past due premiums plus interest within three years, the insurance company must reinstate the policy.

(B) If the company, through its producer, accepts a reinstatement application and issues a conditional receipt, then the policy is automatically reinstated on the 45th day if the insurance company takes no action in the interim.

(C) The insurance company can collect up to 60 days past due premium.

(D) A reinstated policy offers accident coverage immediately and sickness coverage after a 10 day waiting period.

8. Janice has just suffered a loss under her Major Medical Policy. The first step that she must take in the claims process would be stated in which of the following policy provisions?

(A) Claim Forms

(B) Notice of Claim

(C) Payment of Claims

(D) Proof of Loss

9. Harriett has her Major Medical policy reinstated on July 1. On July 8, she suffers a stroke. Harriett will probably receive

(A) Full benefits because her policy has been reinstated.

(B) Residual disability benefits for the duration of her benefit period.

(C) No benefits during her elimination period.

(D) No benefits at all for this loss.

10. The Time Limit on Certain Defenses/Incontestable provision states that the

    (A) Policyowner has the right to sue the insurance company within three years of submitting the proof of loss.
    (B) Company's best defense against a lawsuit concerning a disputed claim is to prove that there was material misrepresentation on the application.
    (C) Policyowner has up to three years to prepare its defense against a lawsuit started by the company.
    (D) Company can challenge paying a claim under the policy based on misstatements made on the application for up to three years (two years in some states) after the policy issue date.

11. Under the Uniform Health Policy Provisions Law, the provision which states that the insurance company has 15 days to send the blank proof of loss forms to the insured is called

    (A) Claim Forms
    (B) Proof of Loss
    (C) Notice of Claim
    (D) Payment of Claims

12. The Time of Payment of Claims provision requires that the company pay income benefits no less frequently than

    (A) Weekly
    (B) Monthly
    (C) Quarterly
    (D) None of the above

13. Uncle Joe, at age 50, intentionally understated his age on an application for a Disability Income policy. Three years later, he had a claim and the insurance company discovered Uncle Joe's true age. The company would probably

    (A) Deny the claim based on intentional and material misrepresentation on the application.
    (B) Deny this claim and issue Uncle Joe a new policy based on his actual age.
    (C) Sue Uncle Joe for fraud and cancel the policy.
    (D) Pay somewhat reduced policy benefits.

© 2017 Pathfinder Corporation

CHAPTER 15
UNIFORM INDIVIDUAL HEALTH POLICY PROVISIONS QUIZ

14. One year ago, Fred purchased a Major Medical Expense Policy. He recently suffered a stroke and incurred $20,000 of medical expenses. The insurance company denied the claim on the basis that its underwriting handbook disallowed paying claims occurring during the first policy year. The provision that would keep the company from using this line of reasoning is called:

(A) Entire Contract; Changes
(B) Payment of Claims
(C) Legal Action
(D) Time Limit on Certain Defenses

15. The mandatory provision which states that the insured has a specified number of days to return the completed claim forms to the insurance company after a loss is called

(A) Claim Forms
(B) Proof of Loss
(C) Time of Payment of Claims
(D) Notice of Claim

16. The Legal Action provision specifies that the insured cannot sue the company until how long after submission of written proof of loss?

(A) 30 days
(B) 45 days
(C) 60 days
(D) 90 days

17. Assume that you purchase an AD&D policy on your spouse and name yourself as the beneficiary. Also assume that you name your child as the individual to receive the benefits if you predecease your spouse. In this situation, your child would be considered the

(A) Tertiary beneficiary
(B) Irrevocable beneficiary
(C) Contingent beneficiary
(D) Primary beneficiary

© 2017 Pathfinder Corporation

15.   B.   Step number three in the claims process: prove the loss.

16.   C.   Window of opportunity to sue: 60 days and 3 years.

17.   C.   Primary beneficiary is first in line to collect. If they die before the insured, then the contingent beneficiary would receive the benefit. Secondary could also work, but it is not a choice.

18.   A.   Only an executive officer of the insurance company is authorized to modify the contract.

© 2017 Pathfinder Corporation

CHAPTER 16
GROUP LIFE

1.   All of the following would qualify for a group insurance plan EXCEPT:

   (A)   10 employees of Mad Marvin's Pizzeria.
   (B)   A group of hypochondriacs formed for the sole purpose of purchasing a group plan.
   (C)   600 members of the Professional Insurance Agents Association of America.
   (D)   Debtors of a local lending institution.

2.   A method of marketing group benefits to employers who have a small number of employees, and which may be fully insured or self-insured is known as a

   (A)   Trade Association
   (B)   MET or MEWA
   (C)   Negotiated Trusteeship
   (D)   TPA

3.   Which of the following plans would NOT be used for insuring the lives or health of employees?

   (A)   Blanket contract
   (B)   KEOGH
   (C)   MET
   (D)   MEWA

4.   A Non-contributory Group Insurance Plan is one in which

   (A)   The employees pay no part of the cost.
   (B)   The employer pays no part of the cost.
   (C)   A payroll deduction plan is used.
   (D)   A waiting period is mandatory.

5. The right of an employee to exchange coverage under group life insurance for an individual policy within 31 days from termination of employment is provided by the

(A) Renewability provision
(B) Conversion provision
(C) Reinstatement provision
(D) COBRA

6. Which of the following is a significant difference between individual policies and Group Life insurance contracts?

(A) Since individual applications are normally taken on each member of a group, group underwriting is more complicated than individual underwriting.
(B) Group underwriting is based on averages, such as the average age, the average working conditions and the average health condition of the group members.
(C) There is more adverse selection in group underwriting than there is in individual underwriting.
(D) Individual Life policies are less likely to lapse.

7. Which of the following statements about group life conversion is NOT true?

(A) Group life insurance plans must offer the insureds the right to convert their dependent coverages to individual policies upon termination of employment.
(B) In Group life plans the insured employee has 31 days from leaving employment to convert to an individual policy.
(C) In Group life plans the parting employee is still covered by the group plan for at least 31 days.
(D) Group life plans must comply with COBRA.

8. The beneficiary of a Group Credit Life policy is the

(A) Creditor
(B) Debtor
(C) Insured
(D) Spouse of the insured

© 2017 Pathfinder Corporation

9.   In Group insurance, the policy is called the

    (A)   Individual Certificate
    (B)   Master Contract
    (C)   Certificate of Insurance
    (D)   Group Plan document

END

QUIZ ANSWERS & EXPLANATIONS ON NEXT PAGE

© 2017 Pathfinder Corporation

CHAPTER 16
GROUP LIFE QUIZ ANSWER KEY

1. B. If we allowed a group of hypochondriacs to buy insurance it would represent Adverse Selection at its worst.

2. B. A MET is simply a group of small employers (who are eligible to buy group insurance) banding together to form a larger group.

3. B. Keogh is a retirement plan.

4. A. In a non-contributory plan, the employer pays the entire premium. The employee does not contribute.

5. B. It permits converting a group life policy to an individual life policy without proof of insurability.

6. B. Group underwriters must consider the characteristics of the entire group.

7. D. COBRA applies to group health insurance, not group life insurance.

8. A. In credit life, the creditor is the owner and the beneficiary of the policy.

9. B. There is only one master contract and the group organizer is the contract owner.

© 2017 Pathfinder Corporation

CHAPTER 17
GROUP HEALTH

1.   The question of Nonduplication and Coordination of Benefits is quite important in group health underwriting. In this regard, which of the following is NOT true?

   (A)   A primary purpose for the Nonduplication and Coordination of Benefits clauses found in group health contracts is to stop the insured from profiting from a loss.
   (B)   The group Coordination of Benefits clause designates the insured's/ claimant's policy as primary and the insured's spouse's policy as excess.
   (C)   The primary carrier must pay as if no other carrier exists. The excess carrier must waive its own deductibles and coinsurance, and pay what the primary carrier did not pay.
   (D)   The primary policy for any insured children will be the policy insuring the older spouse.

2.   You are covered by a Group Major Medical plan at work. Your spouse is also covered by a similar plan by her employer. Both plans have Nonduplication and Coordination of Benefits clauses and both automatically cover the employee's spouse and dependents. You incur a claim for $2000 of covered expenses for which each of the two insurance companies would normally pay $1800. How much would the excess insurance company pay?

   (A) $ 0
   (B) $ 200
   (C) $ 900
   (D) $1800

3.   The federal law that mandates the continuation of group health coverage for insured employees and/or their dependents after a qualifying event is

   (A)   ERISA
   (B)   COBRA
   (C)   CERCLA
   (D)   MEWA

© 2017 Pathfinder Corporation

4.   Assume that you work for XYZ Corporation that provides a full range of employee benefits including group Comprehensive Major Medical and group Disability Income benefits. Which of the following statements about your benefits is true?

(A)   Your group medical expense program provides both occupational and nonoccupational coverages.

(B)   Your group disability income coverages provide both occupational and nonoccupational benefits.

(C)   Group medical expense benefits are coordinated with Worker's Compensation benefits.

(D)   Worker's Compensation provides both occupational and nonoccupational benefits.

5.   Which of the following is true about the tax treatment of group insurance plans?

(A)   The benefits paid under a Major Medical Policy are not taxed as ordinary income.

(B)   The premiums paid by a group policyowner for either Major Medical or for Disability Income protection for the employees are deductible as ordinary business expenses.

(C)   The benefits paid to an employee under a group noncontributory Disability Income contract are taxable as ordinary income to the employee.

(D)   All of the above.

6.   Under COBRA, which of the following situations does not meet the eligibility criteria for continuation of health insurance coverage for an employee or a dependent?

(A)   A forced reduction in hours for the covered employee
(B)   Voluntary resignation of the covered employee
(C)   The covered employee is fired for gross misconduct
(D)   A dependent marries

7.   Under HIPAA, a certificate of prior creditable coverage of 12 months would mean:

(A)   There will be no pre-existing conditions exclusion.
(B)   There will be no co-payment required for covered losses.
(C)   There will be an increased premium.
(D)   The insurance company must cover every loss.

© 2017 **PATHFINDER CORPORATION**

CHAPTER 17
GROUP HEALTH QUIZ ANSWER KEY

1.   D.   The primary policy for children will be the policy of the spouse with a birthday that occurs earliest in the year. Age of the spouse is not a factor.

2.   B.   If you would normally be responsible for $200, as in this question, the secondary policy could pay that amount.

3.   B.   COBRA allows the insured or dependents to continue in the group health plan for a limited time.

4.   B.   Only Disability Income policies can cover both occupational and nonoccupational losses.

5.   D.   All are true. Medical Expense benefits are never taxed. The employer can deduct the cost of premiums for a policy that benefits employees. Benefits paid for a Group Disability Income policy are taxed as ordinary income.

6.   C.   Termination for gross misconduct would not be a trigger event for COBRA.

7.   A.   The 12 month prior creditable service would mean that the insured has already satisfied all pre-existing conditions requirements.

© 2017 Pathfinder Corporation

LIFE REVIEW QUIZ

1. In which required life insurance policy provision would a policyowner find the company's consideration?

    (A) Entire Contract Clause
    (B) Incontestable Clause
    (C) Insuring Clause
    (D) Basic Provisions Clause

2. Which of the following best explains why Extended Term is a nonforfeiture option NOT available to the owner of a rated policy?

    (A) Assignment Clause
    (B) Probationary Period
    (C) It's a unilateral contract
    (D) Adverse Selection

3. You find you have a dividend due you from your Mutual Company. Which of the following is not an option available to you?

    (A) Cash
    (B) Reduced Paid-up
    (C) Paid-up additions
    (D) Reduce next year's premium

4. Ann buys a life insurance policy that gives her the flexibility of changing her death benefit within reason. Her policy also allows her to withdraw money from her cash value without having to repay it. In addition, Ann directs the investment of the cash value. What kind of policy does Ann own?

    (A) A Variable Universal Life Policy
    (B) An Adjustable Life Insurance Policy
    (C) A Variable Whole Life Policy
    (D) A Universal Life Policy

5. Which of the following statements concerning Annuities is false?

(A) Life Annuities will pay you a monthly income for the rest of your life.
(B) Straight Life Annuities provide a larger monthly income than Refund Life Annuities.
(C) An Annuity Certain only pays until age 100.
(D) A Life Annuity with Period Certain pays for life and perhaps beyond.

6. A policyowner has a life insurance policy with cash value. The policyowner fails to pay her premium at the end of the grace period. Coverage does not continue under a nonforfeiture option. Therefore, you know the policyowner has a(n):

(A) Payor Benefit Rider
(B) Accelerated death benefit
(C) Waiver of Premium Rider
(D) Automatic Premium Loan Rider

7. Wiley had a car accident and was hospitalized on his 45th birthday. 89 days later, Wiley died as a result of the accident. Wiley's $100,000 Whole Life policy with a Double Indemnity Rider will:

(A) Pay $200,000
(B) Pay $300,000
(C) Pay only if the settlement option is cash.
(D) Pay $100,000

8. The required life insurance policy provision which guarantees a policy owner's right to secure a loan from their cash value is:

(A) The Ownership Clause
(B) The Insuring Clause
(C) The Loan Provision Clause
(D) The Entire Contract Clause

9. Barry wants to know how the insurance company views the statements he made on his application. After looking over his policy, Barry found that his statements are considered to be representations. Where did Barry find that information?

    (A) Insuring Clause
    (B) Entire Contract Clause
    (C) Ownership Clause
    (D) Assignment Clause

10. Rick bought a life insurance policy in 1967 at the age of 22. His policy stated that the cash value would equal the face amount in 1997. His twin brother Nick bought a policy in 1995 at the age of 50 that will be paid up in 2000. What do the brothers own?

    (A) Rick and Nick both own Whole Life.
    (B) Rick owns a Modified Endowment Contract and Nick owns an Endowment Contract.
    (C) Rick owns an Endowment Contract and Nick owns a Modified Endowment Contract.
    (D) Rick owns Universal Life and Decreasing Term and Nick owns Variable Universal Life and Increasing Term.

11. Which of the following life policies has a protection element of term insurance and cash value that grows on an interest sensitive basis?

    (A) Universal Life
    (B) Renewable Term
    (C) Adjustable Life
    (D) Variable Universal Life

12. Which of the following is true concerning a Life Annuity?

    (A) A physical is normally required before the annuity owner elects an income option.
    (B) The sex of the owner is an important factor in determining premium during the Accumulation Phase.
    (C) The age of the owner is an important factor in determining the monthly income the annuity owner will receive during the Pay Out phase.
    (D) Life Annuities with a Period Certain are not available to owners who are substandard risks.

© 2017 PATHFINDER Corporation

LIFE REVIEW QUIZ

13. A 40-year old woman works, her husband does not. What is the maximum amount the couple may contribute to their IRA(s) annually?

   (A) The maximum contribution into each of two IRAs.
   (B) Half of the maximum contribution into each of two IRAs.
   (C) The maximum contribution into one IRA.
   (D) None of the above.

14. Joe dies in a horrible accident involving a twisted Slinky. Jolene, who was Joe's only beneficiary, can't get over the loss. You see, she really loved that Slinky. 48 days after Joe died, Jolene also passes away. If Joe's death benefit ends up in his estate, it means that:

   (A) The Uniform Simultaneous Death Act dictated it.
   (B) Joe had a Common Disaster Provision in his policy.
   (C) Jolene was a Tertiary Beneficiary.
   (D) Joe forgot to select a settlement option.

15. Under the NAIC Model Provisions, which of the following is not a required life insurance policy provision?

   (A) Insuring Clause
   (B) Assignment Clause
   (C) Premium Payment Clause
   (D) Suicide Clause

16. In the process of selecting and classifying a risk, an underwriter would utilize information found in all of the following EXCEPT the:

   (A) NAIC Buyer's Guide
   (B) MIB Files
   (C) Attending Physician's Report
   (D) Producer's Report

LIFE REVIEW QUIZ

17. Harley Breathing gave his life insurance application and premium to his producer on August 2. There was no interim insuring agreement issued. The insurance company issues the policy and on September 9 the producer shows up at Harley's house with the policy in hand only to find that Harley died in an accident on September 1st. What action will the company take?

    (A) Pay the claim because Harley died during the 30 day Grace Period.
    (B) Pay the claim because Harley's death was an accident.
    (C) Deny the claim because there was no contract.
    (D) Deny the indemnity rider, but pay the face amount of the policy.

18. In which of the following situations would you have to prove that you're insurable?

    (A) You are exercising your option to Convert your Convertible Term Policy to a permanent form of protection.
    (B) You are reinstating your Whole Life Policy
    (C) You are exercising your Guaranteed Insurability Rider option to purchase more insurance.
    (D) Your Variable Whole Life Policy's death benefit needs to be increased to maintain a corridor of safety with the policy's cash value.

19. There are two products specifically designed to allow a young person to purchase a permanent form of protection at a lower initial cost. Those two products are:

    (A) Modified Endowment Contract and Graded Premium Whole Life.
    (B) Reduced Paid-up Whole Life and Level Term.
    (C) Graded Premium Whole Life and Modified Life.
    (D) Modified Life and Modified Endowment.

20. What life insurance product would normally be used to fund a Buy-Sell agreement between two partners of a company?

    (A) Survivorship Life
    (B) Joint Life
    (C) Modified Life
    (D) Business Life

© 2017 PATHFINDER Corporation

21. Fixed, level premiums are ALWAYS a characteristic of:

   (A) Universal Life
   (B) Variable Universal Life
   (C) Variable Whole Life
   (D) Annually Renewable Term

22. If you submit your application and premium money for a life insurance policy and receive a Conditional Receipt, it means your coverage begins:

   (A) On the application date.
   (B) On the date the policy is approved at the home office.
   (C) After an initial 10 day period called the Free Look .
   (D) Later of the application date or physical exam date, if you are insurable as applied for.

23. At age 25, Joe begins accumulating money in his annuity. He pays the same premium amount every year for 40 years. At age 65 Joe annuitizes and selects an annuity that will pay as long as either he or his wife is alive. The annuity pay out is guaranteed in units instead of dollars. What does Joe own?

   (A) A single premium, immediate, refund life annuity.
   (B) A level premium, deferred, variable, joint and survivor life annuity.
   (C) A level premium, immediate, variable life annuity with a period certain.
   (D) A flexible premium annuity certain.

24. All of the following are circumstances that could trigger the paying of an Accelerated Death Benefit EXCEPT:

   (A) Terminal illness of the insured.
   (B) The insured's health requires they be admitted to a nursing home.
   (C) A minor beneficiary of the insured is diagnosed with heart disease.
   (D) The insured has cancer.

END

QUIZ ANSWERS & EXPLANATIONS ON NEXT PAGE

LIFE REVIEW QUIZ
ANSWER KEY

1.   C.   The insurance company's promise to pay, its consideration, is found in the Insuring Clause. Chapter 5.

2.   D.   Adverse Selection is the natural tendency for an insured to select what is best for themselves. If I know that I am dying, I would love to stop paying for my $100,000 Whole Life policy and have it become a $100,000 Term policy. Chapter 6.

3.   B.   The Reduced Paid-up option is a Nonforfeiture option. Chapter 6.

4.   A.   Any Universal Life policy is flexible. Since Ann also has the right to direct the investment of the cash value, it is a Variable Universal contract. Chapter 9.

5.   C.   An Annuity Certain pays only for a designated period of time. Chapter 6.

6.   D.   If the premium is not paid by the end of the Grace Period, then the policy will continue coverage as provided by the Nonforfeiture options unless the policyowner has selected the Automatic Premium Loan option on the application. Chapter 7.

7.   A.   Since the insured died within 90 days of his accident, and the accident is the sole cause of death, AD&D doubles the face amount, or $200,000. Chapter 7.

8.   A.   The Ownership clause states that all policy rights rest with the policyowner, including the right to take policy loans. Chapter 5.

9.   B.   The Entire Contract clause says that statements made on applications are representations. Chapter 5.

10. C.   Rick bought a policy in which the cash value would equal the face value in 30 years, not when Rick reached age 100, so it had to be a 30 Year Endowment policy. Page 4-16. Nick bought a policy that would be paid up in five years, so under the Seven-Pay Rule, this policy would be classified as a Modified Endowment Contract. Chapter 4.

LIFE REVIEW QUIZ ANSWER KEY

11. A. The death benefit in Universal Life is always expressed as Term insurance, and the cash value growth is interest sensitive. Chapter 9.

12. C. Under a Life Annuity payout, since the company is going to pay an income to the annuitant until the annuitant dies, life expectancy is critical. Chapter 4.

13. A. This woman can fully fund her IRA and that of her husband. Chapter 8

14. B. The Common Disaster Provision states that the named beneficiary must outlive the insured by a certain number of days, say 60 days, in order to be eligible to receive the death benefit. Chapter 5.

15. D. The Suicide Clause is an Optional Provision. Chapter 5.

16. A. The Buyer's Guide is information about the relative cost of insurance, which is given to applicants. Chapter 3.

17. C. The only way that a life insurance contract coverage can be put into force without actual delivery is by using an Interim Insuring Agreement. Chapter 2.

18. B. Under the Nonforfeiture Options, in order for the insured to reinstate their policy, they must submit proof of insurability. Chapter 5.

19. C Both Graded Premium Whole Life and Modified Life keep the cost low in the early years of the policy. Chapter 7.

20. B. Joint Life insures two or more individuals and pays upon the death of the first insured. Chapter 7.

21. C. Variable Whole Life is a version of Whole Life. In Whole Life the premiums are always fixed and level. Chapter 4.

22. D. The Conditional Receipt says on the date of the application, or the date of the physical, whichever is later. Chapter 2.

23. B. Same premium = level premium. A 40 year wait for the payout = deferred. A payout in units rather that dollars = variable. Two annuitants = joint and survivorship. Until they are both dead = joint life annuity. Chapter 4.

24. C. The triggers relate to the health condition of the insured, not to the beneficiaries. Chapter 6.

© 2017 Pathfinder Corporation

HEALTH REVIEW QUIZ

1. Which of the following could best summarize the health insurance portfolio of a middle-aged middle class family?

    (A) Medicare and a Medicare Supplement Policy (MSP)
    (B) Medicaid and Long Term Care (LTC)
    (C) Major Medical, Disability Income and LTC
    (D) Disability Income and AD&D

2. AD&D would be best characterized as which of the following?

    (A) A less expensive replacement for a Major Medical policy.
    (B) A specialty product that fits a narrow range of customers at a reasonably low price.
    (C) An essential contract to be properly covered.
    (D) A health insurance policy equivalent to Whole Life or Adjustable Life.

3. Which of the following health policy provisions states what a policyowner gives of value to the insurance company?

    (A) Entire Contract clause
    (B) Renewal clause
    (C) Consideration clause
    (D) Reinstatement clause

4. Which of the following health policies generally can NOT be renewed?

    (A) Individual Disability Income
    (B) LTC
    (C) Flight insurance
    (D) MSP

5. Barry Allen has a Group Major Medical policy at work with a $250 deductible, a 75/25 coinsurance clause and a $10,000 stop loss. There is also a $10,000 AD&D coverage added as a rider. If Barry breaks an arm in a home accident that results in a hospital bill of $2250, his insurance company would pay which of the following?

    (A) $1500
    (B) $2000
    (C) $11,500
    (D) $12,000

6. Tom and Martha Wayne, in their mid 60's, are enjoying their golden years. They live comfortably on their pension checks, government retirement income and the proceeds of a life income being paid by a $400,000 annuity. They have asked you to recommend what health coverages would be appropriate during retirement. You should recommend:

    (A)   Medicaid and LTC
    (B)   Major Medical and Disability Income
    (C)   Medicare Part B , LTC and MSP
    (D)   Medicaid, MSP and SSDI

7. Jennifer Walters, a hard-working gal, wants to purchase a Disability Income policy. In determining Jennifer's benefit limits, you should start with her

    (A)   Gross income.
    (B)   1040 Long Form, line 14.
    (C)   Both earned and unearned income.
    (D)   Earned income.

8. Listed below are the 4 health provisions governing the payment of health claims. What is their proper order?

    1.   Time of Payment of Claims
    2.   Notice of Claim
    3.   Proof of Loss
    4.   Claim Forms

    (A)   2, 3, 1, 4   (C)   4, 3, 2, 1
    (B)   3, 1, 4, 2   (D)   2, 4, 3, 1

© 2017 Pathfinder Corporation

HEALTH REVIEW QUIZ

9. The highest level of guarantee of continuance would most likely be found in which of the following policies?

    (A) Hospital Indemnity
    (B) Medicare Supplement Policies
    (C) Blanket Disability Income
    (D) Dental Care

10. A Disability Income policy would best provide benefits for which of the following?

    (A) Residual Disability
    (B) Catastrophic medical expenses
    (C) Long-Term Care
    (D) Accelerated death benefits

11. Which of the following statements is true concerning an employee's rights under the Group health insurance continuance privilege upon termination of employment?

    (A) HIPAA gives the departing employee the right to convert to an individual policy of health insurance that will continue through some advanced age, such as age 65.
    (B) The departing employee has the right to join a federally-sponsored health insurance pool until coverage can be obtained from a new employer.
    (C) The departing employee has the right to remain in the old employer's group for a limited period of time, such as 18 or 36 months, as defined under COBRA.
    (D) There are no rights of continuance under Group health insurance.

12. In a health insurance policy which of the following most accurately describes the Probationary (Waiting) Period?

    (A) The period of time from the date of the loss until benefits begin.
    (B) The period of time from the date of the loss until benefits are actually received by the policyowner.
    (C) A period of time starting on the policy effective date during which time there is no coverage for claims due to illnesses.
    (D) The period of time once a claim is received by the insurance company before they pay the benefits to the policyowner.

13. Which of the following is true in comparing Medical Expense policies to Disability Income policies?

(A) Medical Expense policies only have one insured whereas Disability Income policies cover the entire family.

(B) Medical Expense policies are written on a valued contract basis whereas Disability Income policies are written on either a service or reimbursement basis.

(C) Medical Expense policies have dollar deductibles whereas Disability Income policies have time deductibles.

(D) Medical Expense policies are written to cover home health care services whereas Disability Income policies require hospitalization.

14. MSPs and LTC policies share many common provisions. Which of the following is NOT a common provision?

(A) 30 Day Free Look
(B) Outline of Coverages
(C) Replacement requirements
(D) Benefits provided

15. John Jones has owned a DI policy for the last 10 years. The annual premium was due on February 1st, but John didn't pay the premium. On February 29th, John was struck by a meteor, but he lived to tell the tale. However, he was disabled for four weeks as a result of the accident and filed a DI claim. Which of the following policy provision(s) may provide a just cause for the company to not pay any benefits?

(A) Elimination Period
(B) Probationary Period
(C) Change of Occupation
(D) Misstatement of Age.

16. Arthur Curry is age 68, jobless, broke and with virtually no assets. Arthur's medical expenses should be paid by

(A) Major Medical and LTC
(B) LTC and MSP
(C) Medicaid and MSP
(D) Medicare and Medicaid

© 2017 Pathfinder Corporation

HEALTH REVIEW QUIZ

17. Which of the following is true regarding health insurance occupational coverages?

   (A)   Group Major Medical policies provide occupational coverages but Group Disability Income policies do not.
   (B)   Group Disability Income policies provide occupational coverages but individual Disability Income policies do not.
   (C)   Both Group Disability Income policies and individual Disability Income policies provide occupational coverages but Group Major Medical does not.
   (D)   As a general rule, neither Group Disability Income nor Group Medical Expense provide coverages for occupational injury.

18. Which of the following is true regarding the rights of dependent children under a Group Major Medical policy written for a family?

   (A)   Adopted children must be covered from the moment of birth.
   (B)   Coverages can not be extended beyond a child's 19th birthday.
   (C)   Disabled children have no rights under Group Major Medical contracts.
   (D)   A new parent has 31 days to notify the insurance company of the birth of a child.

19. Which of the following NAIC model health provisions does NOT contain any key numbers?

   (A)   Reinstatement
   (B)   Legal Action
   (C)   Proof of Loss
   (D)   Change of Occupation

20. Carol Danvers owns a Comprehensive Major Medical policy with a $2000 Base plan, $500 deductible, $500,000 Major Medical lifetime benefit limit with an 80/20 coinsurance clause and a $10,000 stop loss. If Carol has a $2000 covered loss, how much will the insurance company pay?

   (A) $2000
   (B) $1600
   (C) $1500
   (D)   None of the above

© 2017 Pathfinder Corporation

21. Barbara Gordon, age 34, is the proud co-owner of Retro Rocket Remanufacturing Corp. There are two other principal owners. Which of the following policies would you be least likely to recommend to Barbara for her current needs?

    (A)   Long-Term Care
    (B)   Business Overhead Expense
    (C)   Business Disability Buyout
    (D)   Group Disability Income

22. An applicant for a health insurance policy submits a prepaid application and is issued a conditional receipt. Three days later the applicant completes the required medical exam. However, information discovered during the medical exam convinces the underwriter to issue a policy different than the one requested. The producer delivers the policy to the applicant who then pays the additional premium required. The effective date of coverage will be which of the following?

    (A)   The date of the application.
    (B)   The date of the medical exam.
    (C)   The policy issue date.
    (D)   The date of delivery of the policy to the applicant.

23. Which of the following will determine how much you are entitled to in benefits under OASDI?

    (A)   PPO
    (B)   PIA
    (C)   POS
    (D)   NAIC

24. Billy Batson ruined his knees playing basketball in high school. His condition renders him uninsurable to most underwriters. However, there may be a possibility of coverage for the remainder of his body under which of the following riders?

    (A)   Guaranteed Insurability rider
    (B)   Impairment rider
    (C)   Multiple Indemnity rider
    (D)   Easy rider

25.   Which of the following is a significant difference between individual and group health contracts?

(A)   Coinsurance provisions
(B)   Number of insureds
(C)   Use of deductibles
(D)   Types of coverages offered

26.   Assume that you receive benefits from the following policies. Which would always result in a taxable income to you?

(A)   Accidental Death
(B)   Group Major Medical
(C)   Individual Disability Income
(D)   Group non-contributory Disability Income

27.   A producer and an applicant complete an application for a health policy and submit it to the insurance company for underwriting without any premium. The underwriter issues a policy and mails it to the producer for delivery to the applicant. The producer should do all of the following during the delivery of the policy to the applicant EXCEPT:

(A)   Collect the initial premium payment.
(B)   Issue a conditional receipt.
(C)   Have the applicant complete a statement of continued good health.
(D)   Explain the Free Look provision which begins on the policy delivery date.

28.   In most states, laws concerning HIV testing would permit:

(A)   The company to document the sexual orientation of the applicant.
(B)   The company to report the complete results of the test to the MIB.
(C)   Certain exclusions in coverage for HIV or AIDS.
(D)   The test with the applicant's permission.

29.   Grace Periods: _____ days for weekly premium policies. _____ days for monthly. _____ days for all other premium modes.

HEALTH REVIEW QUIZ

30.   Reinstatement: You must wait _____ days for automatic reinstatement.
The company may request up to _____days of past due premium.
Once reinstated, there is a _____day wait for sickness coverage.

31.   Notify your insurance company of a claim within _____days.

32.   You should receive blank Claim Forms within _____days.

33.   You should submit your Proof of Loss to the company within _____days.

34.   Medical Expense claims should be paid _____.

35.   Disability Income claims must be paid no less frequently than _____.

36.   Your window of opportunity for taking Legal Action against your company is
no sooner than _____days and no later than _____ years.

END

QUIZ ANSWERS & EXPLANATIONS ON NEXT PAGE

HEALTH REVIEW QUIZ
ANSWER KEY

1. C. Medicare is for senior citizens, not for the middle-aged. Medicaid is for people who are broke. AD&D is not a primary coverage. The average middle class family has medical expense insurance at work through Major Medical coverage. They need Disability Income protection to cover the potential for loss of income due to accident or sickness. And the risk of needing nursing home coverage is provided by LTC. Chapter 10 & 13

2. B. AD&D is not a primary coverage. It is a specialty limited coverage that only pays for the accidental loss of life or the accidental loss of limbs. Chapter 14.

3. C. Consideration are the things of value that are exchanged between the parties to a contract. In a health policy, the Consideration Clause states that the applicant gives the Company two things of value: the statements made on the application and the payment of the first premium. Chapters 2 & 10.

4. C. Most health policies can be renewed. One exception is Flight Insurance, which is only good for the duration of the flight. Chapter 10.

5. A. AD&D pays for lost arms, but not broken arms. Major Medical will pay for repairing a broken arm. Take the loss of $2250. Subtract the $250 deductible. That leaves $2000. The Company will pay 75% of the $2000 = $1500. Chapter 12.

6. C. Medicare Part A is automatic for Fully Insured individuals over age 65. Medicare Part B is optional and needed. Since Parts A and B together provide about 60% coverage, Tom and Martha will also need a Medicare Supplement Policy to boost the medical expense coverages closer to 90%. Then they will need Long Term Care coverage because Medicare does not provide adequate nursing home coverage. Chapter 13.

7. D. The basis for determining the limits of coverage for Disability Income policies is an applicant's earned income, not their total income or their unearned income. Chapter 11.

8. D. Notice claim forms proof payment. Chapter 15.

© 2017 Pathfinder Corporation

HEALTH REVIEW QUIZ ANSWER KEY

9. B.   MSPs by law must be written on either a Noncancellable or a Guaranteed Renewable basis, which are the two best guarantees of renewability. Chapters 10 & 13.

10. A.   Residual Disability benefits are provided by Disability Income policies. Chapter 11.

11. C.   Be careful to distinguish between Group Life benefits and Group Health benefits! They are different. Health benefits are controlled by COBRA and HIPPA. Group Life continuance benefits are controlled by state conversion rights laws. There is no federally sponsored insurance pool. Chapters 16 & 17.

12. C.   Please differentiate between the Probationary Period and the Elimination Period. The Probationary Period starts on the first day of policy coverage and only occurs once in the life of the policy, while the Elimination Period starts on the date of the loss and occurs every time there is a loss. Pages Chapters 10 & 11.

13. C.   Choice A and B are both just reversed. Chapters 11 & 12.

14. D.   While LTC policies and MSPs share many common provisions, such as Free Looks and mandatory Outlines Of Coverages, they clearly provide different benefits. LTCs cover the cost of nursing homes, while MSPs are medical expense coverages. Chapter 13.

15. A.   Since John pays his DI premium annually, he has a 31 day Grace Period. The premium due date was February 1st. The accident happened on February 29th, so the accident happened during the Grace Period. Therefore, the accident would be covered. So if John were out of work for four weeks, why didn't he receive any benefits? The answer is that John's policy must have an Elimination/Waiting period in excess of four weeks. Chapter 10 & 11.

16. D.   Since Arthur is over age 65, we can assume that he is entitled to Medicare. And since Arthur is over age 65 and broke, we know that he is also entitled to Medicaid. Medicaid will pay for what Medicare won't pay for. Chapter 18.

17.   C.   Occupational coverages refer to those coverages provided to employees by their employers, which would include Group Major Medical, Group Disability Income and Workers Compensation. Workers Comp is medical expense coverage for work related accidents or sicknesses. If you are on the job, it's Workers Comp. If you are not the job, then you are covered by Major Medical. Disability Income policies, whether they are written on an individual or Group basis, cover you both on the job and off the job. Chapter 10.

18.   D.   Adopted children date of placement; natural children moment of birth but there is a notification requirement. Chapter 12.

19.   D.   A, B and C are full of time limits. But D, Change Of Occupation, explains the procedure for adjusting benefits/premiums if the Insured changes to either a more or less hazardous occupation. Chapter 15.

20.   A.   This question is full of unnecessary facts. So what is relevant? The fact that it is a Comprehensive Major Medical plan means that it has a Base Plan up front, which has no deductible and no coinsurance requirement. And the fact that the Base Plan is just big enough to pay the entire $2000 loss. Chapter 12.

21.   A.   Since Barbara is age 34, it is unlikely that she currently needs nursing home coverages. But the other three business related coverages are quite relevant to her today. Chapters 11 & 13.

22.   D.   Since a Conditional Receipt was issued to the applicant, insurance coverage could begin on the date of the application or the date of the medical exam, whichever was later, but only IF the applicant was insurable exactly as applied for. That was not the case in this question. However, the insurance company did make a counter-offer by issuing a policy that was different than the one applied for. The applicant accepted the company's counter-offer by paying the additional premium. Coverage would start at the time of payment of the additional premium. Chapter 2.

23.   B.   Your benefits under Social Security (OASDI) are determined by your PIA, which stands for your Primary Insurance Amount. The PIA is based on your average monthly wage. Chapter 18.

24.   B.   The Impairment Rider allows the insurance company to exclude coverage for one part of an insured's body, such as the insured's knees. Chapter 10.

HEALTH REVIEW QUIZ ANSWER KEY

25. B. The coverages and policy provisions in individual policies and Group policies are very similar. The real difference between the plans is the number of people covered by each: in Group, tens, hundreds or even thousands of people per plan; in individual policies, it is one person or a family. Chapter 16.

26. D. In a Group non-contributory DI policy all of the premium is being paid using before-tax dollars. Therefore, all of the benefits received by the employees are taxable as ordinary income. Chapter 10.

27. B. Since the application was submitted without any premium, a Conditional Receipt could not have been issued. And Conditional Receipts are only issued at the time of application. Chapter 2.

28. D. A company can require AIDS testing, but only with the applicant's written permission. Chapter 3.

29. 7, 10, 31, Weekly, Monthly, Everything Else. Chapter 15.

30. 45, 60 and 10. Chapter 15.

31. 20 Days. Chapter 15.

32. 15 Days. Chapter 15.

33. 90 Days. Chapter 15.

34. Immediately. Chapter 15.

35. Monthly. Chapter 15.

36. 60 Days. Three years. Chapter 15.

© 2017 Pathfinder Corporation

LIFE FINAL EXAM

1. Betty Boop applies for a life insurance policy but does not submit any premium with her application. When will her coverage begin if the company issues the policy?

   (A) On the application date.
   (B) On the date the home office approves her application.
   (C) On the later of either her application date or the date of her medical examination if the policy is issued exactly as Betty applied for it.
   (D) On the date the policy is delivered and she pays the premium and signs a statement of continued good health.

2. In life insurance, the applicant must have an insurable interest

   (A) On the policy renewal date.
   (B) When the policyowner cashes in the policy.
   (C) At the time of a loss.
   (D) At the time of application.

3. Which of the following statements is true about Universal Life?

   (A) The cash value will grow at a guaranteed rate based upon the policyowner's payment of a fixed premium and a locked-in interest rate paid by the company.
   (B) The policyowner may withdraw part of the cash value and never pay it back, which is referred to as a partial surrender .
   (C) After age 59 1/2, the policyowner may withdraw the entire cash value of the policy tax free.
   (D) The policyowner controls where the cash value is invested.

4. As a producer, you take a prepaid application today for a Universal Life policy on Joe Insured. You issue Joe a Conditional Receipt and no medical exam is required. Which of the following actions would you NOT take on this original interview?

   (A) Explain to Joe that the coverage will be effective as of this date if Joe is insurable as applied for.
   (B) Explain to Joe that all promises from the company are contained in the policy.
   (C) Explain to Joe that the 10 day free look provision will commence on the policy delivery date.
   (D) Explain to Joe that the policy will go into effect when it is delivered to him by the producer.

© 2017 Pathfinder Corporation

5. Which of the following statements is NOT true about traditional Whole Life insurance policies?

    (A)   Whole Life policies can either be purchased with a single premium, by installments for a certain number of years, or by payment for the life of the contract.
    (B)   Whole Life policies provide coverage through age 100.
    (C)   Term riders could be added to provide life coverages for a spouse and/or children.
    (D)   The Whole Life policies are always written with flexible premium.

6. Carol Barrick, who is age 30, owns a $200,000 Level Term insurance policy which is Renewable to Age 65 issued by Mackinac Mutual. Which of the following statements about her policy is true?

    (A)   Carol's premium will be the same amount each year through age 65.
    (B)   Carol may renew her policy through age 65 without showing proof of insurability.
    (C)   Carol may increase the face amount of her policy by 10% every 5 years at her option.
    (D)   Carol may convert her term insurance into Whole Life only prior to age 40.

7. A customer submits a prepaid application to an insurance company for a standard rate life policy. Because of the customer's prior health problems, the insurance company will only issue a rated policy. The customer agrees to the higher price and pays the premium. From a contract law point of view, how were the negotiations conducted?

    (A)   Invitation to make an offer, offer, acceptance.
    (B)   Offer, counter-offer, acceptance.
    (C)   Invitation to make an offer, offer, counter-offer, acceptance.
    (D)   Offer, acceptance.

8. Which of the following provisions would be found in a life insurance contract?

    (A)   Change of Occupation
    (B)   Incontestable
    (C)   Probationary Period
    (D)   Elimination Period

9. Which of the following policies use Whole Life and Convertible Term to provide coverage for every member of the family?

   (A) Family (Protection) policy
   (B) Family Income policy
   (C) Family Maintenance policy
   (D) Jumping Juvenile policy

10. The life insurance policy type that provides the policyowner with the greatest control over all elements of the policy, such as the amount of the death benefit, the size of the cash value, and where the cash value is invested is

   (A) Universal Life
   (B) Adjustable Life
   (C) Variable Life
   (D) Variable Universal Life

11. A Single Premium Joint and Survivorship Deferred Variable Life Annuity would have all of the following characteristics EXCEPT:

   (A) The tax deferred accumulation of wealth.
   (B) A tax free death benefit.
   (C) Payments to the annuitant(s) until the last annuitant is deceased.
   (D) To allow the policyowner to invest in the stock market through a family of funds.

12. In which of the following forms of life insurance is the protection always expressed in the form of Term insurance?

   (A) Variable Life
   (B) Universal Life
   (C) Adjustable Life
   (D) Graded Premium Life

13. You wish to give an insurance company $300,000 today and in return you want the company to pay you and your spouse a fixed number of dollars of income per month for the rest of your lives starting 10 years from now. Which of the following would NOT be appropriate to describe this annuity contract?

   (A) Deferred
   (B) Single Premium
   (C) Joint and Survivorship
   (D) Variable

© 2017 Pathfinder Corporation

14. Assume that you own an Adjustable Life Insurance Policy. Which of the following factors can you NOT adjust?

   (A)   The face amount.
   (B)   Where the cash value is invested.
   (C)   The premium.
   (D)   The type of plan (essentially whether you wish to have Term or Whole Life or some combination of the two).

15. Jim S. Broke applied for a life insurance policy two weeks ago and has just been denied coverage because of information the insurance company obtained from a consumer credit report. According to the Fair Credit Reporting Act, all the following statements are true EXCEPT:

   (A)   The insurance company must disclose to Jim the name of the credit reporting agency that issued the report.
   (B)   Jim has the right to obtain a copy of his credit report from the insurance company.
   (C)   The reporting agency may not issue a report containing adverse information that is more than 7 years old (10 years in the case of bankruptcy).
   (D)   Jim may file a statement of dispute with the credit reporting agency to be put in his file.

16. Jolene has a typical double indemnity rider on her $150,000 Whole Life policy. If she dies of a stroke, which of the following is true concerning her coverages?

   (A)   Her policy will pay a $450,000 death benefit.
   (B)   Her policy will pay a $300,000 death benefit.
   (C)   Her policy will pay a $150,000 death benefit.
   (D)   Her policy will pay nothing.

17. Paul Sorrow purchased a typical $250,000 Ordinary Life policy six months ago that contains a two year suicide clause. If Paul were to commit suicide today, his policy would pay which of the following to his beneficiary?

   (A) $250,000
   (B) $250,000 less any outstanding loans.
   (C)   Return of cash value less any outstanding loans.
   (D)   Return of premium paid less any outstanding loans.

© 2017 Pathfinder Corporation

18. Molly was insured under ABC corporation's noncontributory Group Life insurance plan for $30,000. Molly left ABC Company on July 1 and stated to her ex-employer that she had no intention of converting her group coverage. Molly died on July 4. Molly's beneficiary will receive

(A) Flowers
(B) $30,000
(C) A $30,000 life insurance policy
(D) Nothing

19. The clause in a life insurance policy which states that neither party to the contract can unilaterally introduce modifications to the contract is called the

(A) Entire Contract
(B) Incontestable
(C) Reinstatement
(D) Adhesion

20. Harold owns a $400,000 life insurance policy on his own life and has named his wife Gertrude as his primary beneficiary. The secondary beneficiary was Harold's now deceased older sister. Unfortunately, Gertrude and Harold decided to take their second honeymoon on the good ship Titanic, which sank. Both went down with the ship and no one knows who died first. The $400,000 will be paid to which of the following?

(A) Harold's deceased sister's estate.
(B) Gertrude's estate.
(C) Harold's estate.
(D) The American Bar Association.

21. Which of the following settlement options would provide an annuitant with the largest monthly income from a life insurance death benefit?

(A) Straight Life Annuity
(B) Life Annuity with 10 Year Certain
(C) Refund Life Annuity
(D) Joint and Survivorship Life Annuity

22.   Which of the following is true of a Whole Life policy that is continuing under the Waiver of Premium with Disability Income rider as the result of the disability of the policyowner/insured?

(A)   The cash values will continue to grow, but at a slower rate.
(B)   Loan values will be unavailable to the policyowner.
(C)   If declared, dividends will be paid as usual.
(D)   The Reduced Paid-Up and Extended Term nonforfeiture options will be unavailable.

23.   Which of the following variables is NOT considered in determining how much an annuitant would receive under an annuity payout?

(A)   The insurability of the annuitant.
(B)   The age and sex of the annuitant.
(C)   The value of the annuity when it is annuitized.
(D)   The number of lives to be covered.

24.   Twenty years ago Lois Lane and Clark Kent each purchased a Level Premium Annuity. The annuities were identical. Today, each is the same age when they elect to annuitize their contracts.   Both contracts have a $300,000 cash value and both annuitants have chosen the Life Income with 10 Year Period Certain option. All of the following are true EXCEPT:

(A)   Lois and Clark both paid the same premium during the accumulation phase.
(B)   Lois and Clark both will receive the same monthly income amount.
(C)   Both annuities could pay out in excess of $300,000.
(D)   If Lois were to die 15 years from now, the company would have no further obligation under her contract; likewise for Clark's if he were to die 15 years from now.

25.   Which of the following life insurance riders would NOT require additional premium?

(A)   Automatic Premium Loan
(B)   Guaranteed Insurability
(C)   Waiver of Premium
(D)   Return of Premium

26.   Which of the following is NOT a characteristic of a qualified retirement plan?

(A)   The plan may not discriminate in favor of a particular group of employees.
(B)   The plan must be for the exclusive benefit of the employees or their beneficiaries.
(C)   The plan must be funded by federal government guaranteed investments.
(D)   It must be formalized in writing.

27.   Which of the following is NOT a qualified retirement plan?

(A)   Split Dollar
(B)   401 K
(C)   403 B
(D)   Keogh (HR10)

28.   Which of the following is a typical exclusion found in life insurance policies written today?

(A)   Pre-existing Conditions
(B)   Workers Compensation claims
(C)   Suicide after two years
(D)   None of the above

29.   ABC life insurance company is a member of the MIB. As a member, ABC would be required to report all of the following types of applicant information to the MIB EXCEPT:

(A)   Amount of insurance applied for.
(B)   Reckless driving habits.
(C)   Aviation or hazardous sports activities.
(D)   Specific impairments discovered.

30.   Which of the following qualified retirement plans would you recommend for a 501C corporation?

(A)   SIMPLE
(B)   403B
(C)   HR10
(D)   SEP/IRA

31. All of the following are normally part of a Whole Life insurance policy EXCEPT the

   (A)   Nonforfeiture values.
   (B)   Settlement options.
   (C)   Expiration date.
   (D)   Copy of the application.

32. Producer Ima Harry takes a prepaid application for a Universal Life policy from client Weird Willy. The policy is issued and delivered as requested. Six weeks later, Weird dies. The company then discovers some unanswered questions on Weird's application. The company will do which of the following?

   (A)   Refuse to pay the death benefit because of willful and material concealment on the application.
   (B)   Contest the payment of the death benefit.
   (C)   Pay the claim.
   (D)   Protect its rights to obtain the missing information as granted it under the Incontestable Clause.

33. Which of the following is a policyowner NOT required to do to reinstate a Whole Life policy?

   (A)   Pay rates based on the insured's attained age at reinstatement.
   (B)   Pay all past due premium.
   (C)   Provide proof of insurability.
   (D)   Pay interest on all past due premium.

34. As a Producer, you are taking an application from Joe for a $200,000 Variable Universal Life contract on his wife Jolene. Joe plans to be the policyowner and the primary beneficiary. Joe also wishes to name his son, Joe College, age 19, as the secondary beneficiary. All the following individuals should sign the application EXCEPT:

   (A)   You
   (B)   Joe
   (C)   Jolene
   (D)   Joe College

35. Congratulations! You are approaching retirement and are fully insured. Which of the following will be the primary factor in determining how much you will receive as a social security retirement benefit?

    (A)   Your number of dependents.
    (B)   The number of years that you have paid into the Social Security system.
    (C)   Your average monthly wage during your earning years.
    (D)   The size of the Federal government deficit.

36. A judge orders a divorced father to purchase life insurance on his life for the benefit of his dependent children. In order to protect the interests of the children, the judge would most likely order the beneficiaries to be named on which of the following bases?

    (A)   Joint and Survivorship
    (B)   Revocable
    (C)   Irrevocable on a reversionary basis
    (D)   Incontestable

37. Interest sensitive Whole Life generally has all of the following characteristics EXCEPT:

    (A)   The cash value can earn interest at a rate higher than the guaranteed rate.
    (B)   The policyowner's premium and/or death benefit can be adjusted from time to time based on the insurance company's actual risk and expense experience.
    (C)   The cash values are invested in the company's general account.
    (D)   You must hold an NASD license to market Interest sensitive Whole Life policies.

38. The premiums for which of the following types of life insurance are tax deductible as an ordinary business expense to your business?

    (A)   Non-contributory Group
    (B)   Key Employee/Person
    (C)   Buy and Sell
    (D)   Cross Purchase

39. All of the following statements are true concerning the taxation of Whole Life policies EXCEPT:

   (A) Dividends paid by Mutual companies to their policyowners are not taxable.
   (B) Under the Accumulate at Interest option, the interest is taxable in the year in which it is earned.
   (C) Death benefits received by corporations from policies they own on key employees are usually not taxed as income.
   (D) Dividends paid by stock companies to their stockholders are not taxable.

40. Which of the following statements is NOT a characteristic of Universal Life insurance?

   (A) They offer very flexible premium payments.
   (B) Partial surrenders are permitted.
   (C) The cash values can be withdrawn from the policy after age 70 1/2 tax free.
   (D) They are generally written on an interest-sensitive basis.

41. Joe Insured owns a Whole Life policy on his own life with a Guaranteed Insurability rider. Joe has the right to purchase specified additional amounts of insurance

   (A) At specified times in the future at the premium rate of his original policy.
   (B) To cover a newborn without proof of insurability.
   (C) At a specified interval of time for his wife, Jolene, without proof of insurability.
   (D) For himself in the future without proof of insurability but at rates for his attained age.

© 2017 Pathfinder Corporation

42. Which of the following is a reason your premium would increase if you converted your 5 year old Term insurance policy to Whole Life?

    (A)   Converting to Whole Life is an example of adverse selection.

    (B)   The Whole Life premium will be calculated on your attained age, not on the age you were when the Term policy was issued.

    (C)   The face amount of the contract will increase above the guaranteed minimum death benefit depending on the rate of return earned on the cash value.

    (D)   The Whole Life mortality tables are less accurate than the Term mortality tables.

43. A life insurance policy that accumulates cash value at a known rate, provides a constant level of death protection, has a lower premium in the early years of the policy life and a higher premium in the later years of the policy life, is called

    (A)   Graded Premium Whole Life

    (B)   Adjustable Life

    (C)   Universal Life

    (D)   Variable Life

44. Professor Higgins is a self-employed linguist who earns $80,000 per year. Every year he puts aside $8,000 in a Keogh plan. Eliza Dolittle, his secretary, is age 35 and has been employed full-time by the professor for four years. Eliza's salary is $25,000 per year. Which of the following is true regarding Eliza's retirement account?

    (A)   Professor Higgins must deduct $8,000 a year from Eliza's salary for her Keogh plan.

    (B)   Professor Higgins must place $8,000 a year from his income into a Keogh for Eliza.

    (C)   Professor Higgins must deduct $2,500 a year from Eliza's salary for her Keogh plan.

    (D)   Professor Higgins must place $2,500 a year from his income into a Keogh for Eliza.

45. Popeye owns a $100,000 Straight Life policy with a cash value of $9,000 and a $5,000 outstanding loan (including interest). If Popeye dies, his beneficiary, Olive Oyl, will receive

    (A) $104,000

    (B) $100,000

    (C) $ 95,000

    (D)   None of the above

46. In question number 45 above, if Popeye surrenders his policy, how much will he receive?

    (A) $100,000
    (B) $ 9,000
    (C) $ 5,000
    (D) $ 4,000

47. Assume that you own a $100,000 Whole Life policy with a cash value of $11,000. Also assume that you have made a collateral assignment of the policy to Acme Loan Company for an installment loan of $7,000. Which of the following is true?

    (A)   If you die, Acme is entitled to receive the full death benefit as repayment of the loan.
    (B)   If you repay the loan, the collateral assignment will be cancelled, and all policy rights will revert to you.
    (C)   Acme could name itself as the irrevocable beneficiary under the policy.
    (D)   Acme's lien against the policy will remain at $7000 until the loan is fully paid, regardless of the balance at death.

48. Which of the following is an example of third party ownership?

    (A)   403(B)
    (B)   IRA
    (C)   401(K)
    (D)   Group Life

49. Which of the following is true of Group Life insurance?

    (A)   A contributory group is defined as a group in which the employer pays the entire premium.
    (B)   In Group Credit Life, the designated beneficiary is the policyowner.
    (C)   The Conversion privilege allows departing group members to continue their membership in the Group Life plan for either 18 or 36 months.
    (D)   The conversion privilege expires after 10 days.

50. In addition to your life license, to sell Variable Contracts, you must be licensed with the

    (A) NAIC
    (B) AARP
    (C) NASD or SEC
    (D) AMA or AAA

51. Ten years ago, Tim purchased a 20 Pay Life policy with Automatic Premium Loan. Tim failed to pay his premium which was due yesterday. Which of the following statements is true?

    (A) If Tim does not pay his premium before the grace period runs out, the insurance company will put his policy on Extended Term, assuming his policy is not rated.
    (B) If Tim dies tomorrow, his beneficiary will be paid the full death benefit, minus the overdue premium and interest.
    (C) If the insurance company implements the Automatic Premium Loan provision, Tim will be able to regain full cash value of the policy as long as he can meet the Reinstatement requirements.
    (D) The Automatic Premium Loan provision works only if Tim is disabled.

52. On February 2, 1996 Mrs. Abramowitz pays an annual premium of $200 on her $10,000 face value Whole Life policy. Mrs. Abramowitz failed to pay her next premium that was due on February 2, 1997. If Mrs. Abramowitz died on February 19, 1997, her beneficiary/estate would receive, disregarding interest, how much?

    (A) $ 0
    (B) $10,000
    (C) $ 9,800
    (D) None of the above

53. Which of the following events can result in the policyowner receiving cash from an insurance company?

    (A) Payment of policy dividends.
    (B) Electing the Extended Term option.
    (C) Selecting the Automatic Premium Loan option.
    (D) Selecting the Reduced Paid-Up option.

54.   Accelerated Death Benefits

   (A)   Require the insurer to pay the death benefit to the beneficiary within
          thirty days if the insured dies within ninety days of an accident.
   (B)   Allow the insured to surrender the policy and receive the entire cash
          value tax free.
   (C)   Are synonymous with a Living Will.
   (D)   Allow the insurance company to pay a percentage of the death benefit
          to a terminally ill insured.

55.   Which of the following is NOT true of Joint Life insurance?

   (A)   It is an excellent funding vehicle for a Buy and Sell Agreement.
   (B)   It pays the death benefit upon the death of the second or last insured
          to die.
   (C)   It matures upon the death of the first insured.
   (D)   It is less expensive than purchasing an individual policy on each of
          the insureds.

56.   Survivorship Life insurance is

   (A)   Useful in estate planning situations where there are substantial taxes
          to be paid.
   (B)   Usually written with Decreasing Term insurance.
   (C)   Primarily designed to pay a monthly benefit throughout the lifetime of
          one or more annuitants until the last one dies.
   (D)   Usually issued in connection with Juvenile life insurance and allows
          for the waiver of premium in case of the payor's death.

57.   The IRS defines any cash value life insurance policy in which the cash value
       grows faster than a 7 Pay Whole Life policy as a/an

   (A)   Endowment
   (B)   Modified Endowment
   (C)   Modified Life
   (D)   Accelerated Death Benefit

LIFE FINAL EXAM

58. If Joe were to die ten years after purchasing a 20-Pay Whole Life policy, for which of the following reasons could the insurance company deny payment of the death benefit?

    (A) Misstatement of age
    (B) Suicide
    (C) Material misrepresentation on the application
    (D) None of the above

59. A Free Look Provision:

    (A) Means insurance will be given to the applicant free of charge for one policy year.
    (B) Gives the insured the right to return a policy for a full refund.
    (C) Only exists if a policy has cash value.
    (D) Gives the insurer the right to contest statements on an application for up to two years.

60. Which of following is true of a Whole Life policy surrendered for its cash value by the policyowner at age 58?

    (A) Taxes and penalties
    (B) No taxes
    (C) Taxes on the gain
    (D) Taxes on premiums paid

61. A renewable Term insurance policy on which the renewal premium rate will be slightly reduced if the insured can pass a physical exam and will submit a renewal application is called

    (A) Modified
    (B) Re-entry
    (C) Decreasing Premium
    (D) Convertible

62. Which of the following events will NOT generate taxable income?

    (A) Receipt of a policy dividend
    (B) Receipt of a stock dividend
    (C) Surrender of a cash value life insurance policy
    (D) Surrender of a Variable Annuity

© 2017 Pathfinder Corporation

63.   Which of the following is NOT a Nonforfeiture option?

(A)   Reduced Paid-Up
(B)   Reduction of Premium
(C)   Extended Term
(D)   Cash

64.   Which of the following can be sold by a Producer who does NOT also have an NASD/SEC license?

(A)   Variable Annuities
(B)   Adjustable Life
(C)   Mutual Funds
(D)   Variable Universal Life

65.   According to IRS rules, which of the following is true of a cash value policy that you pay up in full in seven or less years?

(A)   It is illegal.
(B)   It will be classified as a MEC and may be subjected to certain negative tax consequences.
(C)   Death benefits paid to a beneficiary will be taxed as ordinary income.
(D)   The policy will be classified as a securities investment.

66.   The Life Insurance Solicitation Regulation, Rule 24, requires that

(A)   The applicant be given adequate information regarding the relative cost of various insurance products.
(B)   All insureds under a group plan be given full disclosure as to the cost of insurance.
(C)   The applicant be given a Buyer's Guide specifically designed for the policy which is the subject of the transaction.
(D)   Medical examinations be scheduled within 30 days of the date of application.

67. As a producer, which of the following best describes your duties under the Replacement Regulation, Rule 16.1?

    (A)   To personally notify the producer who sold the policy which is being replaced.

    (B)   To inform the applicant of their 10 day Free Look under the new policy.

    (C)   To conduct a reasonable investigation as to whether replacement will take place as the result of the purchase of a new policy.

    (D)   To prepare a spreadsheet comparing the old and new coverages as part of the Policy Summary.

68. Which of the following is true regarding the Replacement Regulation, Rule 16.1?

    (A)   Rule 16.1 prohibits the replacement of policies which have been in force for longer than the Incontestable Period.

    (B)   Rule 16.1 limits the number of times that replacement may take place.

    (C)   The underlying purpose of Rule 16.1 is simply to make sure that an individual has enough information to make a valid decision regarding replacement.

    (D)   Rule 16.1 requires that all new policies have the same or better benefits than the policies that they are replacing.

69. Which of the following is true about Living Benefit Agreements?

    (A)   They provide nursing home patients with a disability income benefit after a 5 month waiting period.

    (B)   The term is used interchangeably with the term Living Will.

    (C)   They provide for the payment of the full face amount of the life insurance policy by the insurance company to the Policyowner/ Insured if the insured becomes terminally ill.

    (D)   They permit a policyowner/insured who is suffering from a terminal illness to sell their life insurance to a third party at a price somewhat less than the expected death benefit.

70. Linda is purchasing a new Universal Life policy. Replacement would be involved in all of the following situations EXCEPT

    (A)   Linda will terminate an existing Term to Age 65 policy.

    (B)   Linda will place an existing Whole Life policy on Extended Term.

    (C)   Linda will allow a one year Term policy to expire.

    (D)   Linda will borrow 35% of the cash value of her existing Whole Life policy to purchase the new Universal Life policy.

© 2017 Pathfinder Corporation

71. A Temporary insurance Producer's license

(A) Is intended to be used by new recruits until they have the opportunity to complete their prelicensing education
(B) Authorizes the licensee to solicit new clients.
(C) Only requires that the applicant pass the limited license examination.
(D) May be issued for periods not exceeding 180 days.

72. All of the following may currently obtain a Limited Insurance License without taking an examination EXCEPT:

(A) A person selling baggage insurance in a transportation terminal.
(B) A person selling limited travel accident insurance in a transportation terminal.
(C) A person selling title insurance.
(D) Funeral directors who sell pre-need funeral policies.

73. As a resident insurance Producer you must do all of the following EXCEPT

(A) Pay your license renewal fee as required.
(B) Keep your commissions earned from controlled business to 25% or less of your total commission income.
(C) Live in Indiana.
(D) Notify the Commissioner of any change in residential or business address within 30 days of the change.

74. You offer to give your prospect 25% of your commission if she purchases insurance from you.

(A) This is an example of Controlled Business
(B) This is a violation of the Unfair Competition Law.
(C) This is allowed if the rebate has been filed with the Department of Insurance.
(D) This is allowed if the proper disclosures are filed prior to the time the transaction occurs.

75. All of the following are true statements regarding the Indiana Insurance Commissioner EXCEPT

    (A) He is the chief executive and administrative officer of the Department of Insurance.
    (B) He is a gubernatorial appointee serving a four year term.
    (C) He is chosen on the basis of his knowledge of the subject of insurance, irrespective of his political beliefs or affiliations.
    (D) He is authorized to attend and participate in the annual convention of the National Association of Insurance Commissioners.

76. Which of the following persons would NOT be required to be licensed as a Producer?

    (A) An insurance Producer's secretary who explains routine coverages and quotes premiums to potential customers over the telephone.
    (B) A new recruit who recites a memorized sales presentation to a potential client but does not sign the application or receive any commission or payment.
    (C) A finance manager in an automobile dealership who asks a new car buyer if she would like to have him include insurance in the car loan.
    (D) An insurance company president whose responsibilities consist solely of management and administration of the company.

77. Under Indiana law, which of the following is considered to be an alien insurer?

    (A) An insurance company domiciled in Toronto, Canada.
    (B) An insurance company domiciled in Fort Wayne, Indiana.
    (C) An insurance company domiciled in San Juan, Puerto Rico.
    (D) An insurance company domiciled in Boston, Massachusetts.

78. As a licensed producer, all of the following transactions constitutes controlled business EXCEPT

    (A) Insurance you sell on property owned by your father.
    (B) A policy you sell to your employer.
    (C) Coverage you place on friends.
    (D) Coverage you place on your own property.

© 2017 Pathfinder Corporation

79. As a licensed Producer, you must notify the Commissioner of a change in business or residential address within how many days of the change?

(A)   10
(B)   30
(C)   31
(D)   90

80. All of the following individuals would be exempt from taking an Indiana licensing examination in whole or in part EXCEPT

(A)   An individual who has obtained a CLU and is applying for a Life license.
(B)   A licensed resident producer of another state which has reciprocity with Indiana who wishes to obtain an Indiana nonresident license.
(C)   A producer who is less than 30 days late in renewing their license.
(D)   A funeral director applying for a limited lines license to sell burial insurance.

81. The Commissioner may grant a Temporary license to all of the following individuals EXCEPT

(A)   An applicant who is unable to sit for the licensing examination due to a permanent and total disability.
(B)   Someone designated by a licensed Producer if the Producer is entering active service in the armed forces of the United States.
(C)   The surviving spouse of a recently deceased licensed Producer.
(D)   An employee of a recently disabled licensed Producer.

82. As a licensed Producer, you may do all of the following EXCEPT

(A)   Sell policies and earn commissions on policies issued by admitted companies.
(B)   Hold a Consultant's license.
(C)   Assign your commission to your employing company if you are salaried and the company is also licensed as a Producer.
(D)   Write insurance on yourself or your family as long as no more than 25% of your commission income in any 12 month period comes from it.

© 2017 Pathfinder Corporation

LIFE FINAL EXAM

83. All of the following are defined as unfair methods of competition EXCEPT

   (A) Charging varying premium rates to individuals in different insuring classes.
   (B) Offering to pay the first premium on a policy you sell to a new client.
   (C) Offering to give stock not specified in the policy as an inducement in the purchase of a policy of insurance.
   (D) Delivering an insurance policy entitled Investment Plan.

84. The Commissioner of Insurance has:

   (A) Some of the powers vested in the judicial branch of government.
   (B) Some of the powers vested in the executive branch of government.
   (C) Some of the powers vested in the legislative branch of government.
   (D) Some of the powers vested in all three branches of government.

85. The process by which the Commissioner is given the authority to inspect the financial affairs of any insurer doing business or proposing to do business in Indiana is called

   (A) Examination
   (B) Restitution
   (C) Rehabilitation
   (D) Reformation

86. The Commissioner must post a faithful performance bond in the sum of at least

   (A) $5,000
   (B) $50,000
   (C) $500,000
   (D) $5,000,000

87. To license a business entity as an insurance producer:

   (A) The business entity must be organized as a corporation.
   (B) All employees of the business entity must be individually licensed producers.
   (C) Any employee must be appointed as a compliance officer.
   (D) An employee who holds a producer's license must be appointed as a compliance officer.

© 2017 Pathfinder Corporation

88.   A legally licensed Producer may

(A)   Offer advice for a fee and write coverage for the same client in the
same transaction with adequate disclosure.
(B)   Be licensed as a Consultant.
(C)   Charge a fee for the time spent working on a proposal only if the client
decides not to buy the insurance.
(D)   Share a commission with the Consultant who referred a client to him.

89.   Which of the following would NOT be a violation of the Unfair Claims Settlement
Practices regulations?

(A)   Refusing to pay a claim before conducting a reasonable investigation.
(B)   Failure to settle a claim in a reasonable manner.
(C)   Failure to pay a death claim within 10 days of receipt of proof of
death.
(D)   Failure to acknowledge claim coverage within a reasonable time after
submission of proof of loss.

90.   All of the following must be found in the Policy Summary EXCEPT

(A)   The date the Policy Summary was prepared.
(B)   A listing of the current investment portfolio of the company.
(C)   The Equivalent Level Annual Dividend and a statement that dividends
are not guaranteed.
(D)   The policy loan interest rate.

91.   Which of the following is NOT true of Viatical companies in Indiana?

(A)   They must be licensed by the Department of Insurance.
(B)   They must pay the full face value of any life insurance contracts they
purchase.
(C)   They must obtain the insured's medical records.
(D)   They must provide a 30 day unconditional right of recession to the
insured.

© **2017 PATHFINDER CORPORATION**

92. Which of the following is NOT considered to be replacement of life insurance?

(A) You do not ask and the client does not volunteer the information that he is canceling his existing policy to buy yours.
(B) You are replacing a policy issued by your own company.
(C) You are replacing a Term to 65 policy with a Whole Life policy.
(D) The policyowner is keeping his existing coverage; however, he plans to borrow 20% of the cash value to pay the initial premium on his new policy that he is purchasing from you.

93. All of the following are true concerning Group life insurance EXCEPT that

(A) The designated beneficiary cannot be the employer.
(B) Individual proof of insurability can be required for any member of the group.
(C) All departing employees have a 31 day conversion period.
(D) If a departing employee is not properly informed of the conversion period, then the employee has an additional 90 days to convert to an individual policy.

94. Interest must be paid by a life insurance company on a death benefit if it is not paid within how many days of the submission of valid proof of death?

(A) 10
(B) 15
(C) 30
(D) 60

95. Death benefits must be paid within

(A) 30 days of death.
(B) 30 days of receipt of proof of death.
(C) 2 months of death.
(D) 2 months of receipt of proof of death.

96. When a third party purchases the rights to the proceeds of a life insurance policy covering a terminally ill person, this is referred to as a(n)

(A) Accelerated Death Benefit
(B) 403(b) annuity
(C) Viatical settlement
(D) pre-need benefits plan

© 2017 Pathfinder Corporation

LIFE FINAL EXAM

97. Under Indiana Law, Rules are not

   (A)   Promulgated
   (B)   Passed by the legislature
   (C)   Interpretations of statutes
   (D)   Binding

98. Should a life insurance benefit not be paid in a timely manner, interest

   (A)   Begins to accrue 2 months after the death of the insured.
   (B)   Begins to accrue 30 days after the death of the insured.
   (C)   Accrues at a rate equal to the inflation rate under the CPI.
   (D)   Accrues at a rate equal to the policy loan rate.

99. Which of the following individuals represent terminally ill parties wishing to enter into a viatical settlement?

   (A)   Viators
   (B)   Viatical Producers
   (C)   Viatical Brokers
   (D)   Insurance Consultants

100. Under the Life Insurance Solicitation Regulation, Rule 24, cost is defined as

   (A)   Gross Premium, plus commission.
   (B)   Gross Premium less commission.
   (C)   The difference between what you put in and what you get out.
   (D)   The greater of cash value or the premium paid.

END

EXAM ANSWERS & EXPLANATIONS ON NEXT PAGE

© 2017 Pathfinder Corporation

LIFE FINAL EXAM
ANSWER KEY

1. D. An application without premium is an invitation. The issuance and delivery is the offer. The payment of the premium is the acceptance. Chapter 2.

2. D. Only the applicant needs an insurable interest, and only at the time of application. Chapter 2.

3. B. While Whole Life policies do not allow for a partial surrender of the cash value, Universal Life policies do. Chapter 9.

4. D. With a Conditional receipt, coverage begins later of the date of the application or medical exam if the policy is issued as applied for. Chapter 2.

5. D. Just the opposite is true: The premiums for Whole Life policies are fixed and NOT flexible. It is the premium payment for Universal Life that is flexible. Chapter 4.

6. B. The renewability feature of Term Life allows the insured to renew their policy WITHOUT proving insurability, but at a rate based upon the new attained age. Chapter 4.

7. B. A prepaid application is an offer. The company's willingness to issue a rated policy is a counter-offer. And the applicant's willingness to pay for the rated policy is the acceptance. Chapter 2.

8. B. While both Life and Health policies have Incontestable clauses, the other three provisions are only found in Health policies. Chapter 5.

9. A. If you add Convertible Term riders on the spouse and each of the children, you have just created a Family (Protection) policy. Chapter 7.

10. D. Only Variable Universal Life gives the policyowner control over the death benefit, cash value and how the cash value is invested. Chapter 9.

11. B. Annuities do NOT have tax free death benefits. Any benefits paid under an annuity contract are subject to taxes. Chapter 4.

12. B. The death benefit of Universal Life is Term insurance. Chapter 9.

LIFE FINAL EXAM ANSWER KEY

13. D. The fixed number of dollars of income per month feature of the benefit means that the Annuity type is Fixed or Conventional, not Variable. Chapter 4.

14. B. If the policyowner could adjust where the cash value is invested, it would be a Variable contract, and there is no Variable version of Adjustable Life insurance. Chapter 9.

15. B. Jim can obtain a copy of his credit report from the Credit Bureau that actually collects the credit information, NOT from his insurance company. Chapter 3.

16. C. A Double Indemnity rider only pays if the death was due to an accident. Since Jolene died of a stroke, which is a sickness, only the face amount would be paid. Chapter 7.

17. D. Paul committed suicide during the suicide no pay period, so the insurance company will not pay the death benefit. However, the company will return his premium less any outstanding loans. Chapter 5.

18. B. Death during the conversion is considered death while a member of the group. Chapter 16.

19. A. It would be unfair for one of the two parties to a contractual agreement to have the right to change the agreement without the consent of the other party. Chapter 5.

20. C. Under the Uniform Simultaneous Death Act if an Insured dies at the same time as their beneficiary, we always assume that the beneficiary died first. Chapter 5.

21. A. The fewer guarantees the larger the payment, the Straight/Pure Life Annuity. Chapter 4.

22. C. There is NO reduction in policy benefits if an insured is continuing coverage under the Waiver of Premium benefit. Chapter 7.

23. A. Since the company is paying until you die, they don't care if you are healthy. They probably prefer that you be unhealthy. Chapter 4.

24. B. Lois and Clark will NOT receive the same monthly income because, statistically, Lois will live longer than Clark. Therefore her money must be stretched out further than Clark's money. Chapter 4.

© 2017 Pathfinder Corporation

LIFE FINAL EXAM ANSWER KEY

25. A. The one that does NOT increase the company's risk and benefits the company as much as the insured. Chapter 7.

26. C. Qualified retirement plans are usually funded with mutual funds or individual stocks and bonds, not necessarily with government guaranteed investments. Chapter 8.

27. A. Split-dollar plans are nonqualified. Chapter 8.

28. D. The Exclusions listed in this question are health insurance Exclusions, not life insurance Exclusions. (A preexisting condition in Life insurance would be that the applicant is already dead.) Chapter 10.

29. A. The MIB files contain information that shows you to be an above-average risk, not typical underwriting data, such as the amount of insurance applied for. Chapter 3.

30. B. 501C's get 403B's. Chapter 8

31. C. Whole Life policies either mature at age 100 or upon the death of the insured. They do NOT have expiration dates. Chapter 4.

32. C. With an incomplete application the company has waived the right to the answers. Chapter 2.

33. A. Your age on a reinstated policy is the same as it was before the policy lapsed. Chapter 6.

34. D. The applicant, the proposed insured, and the producer all must sign the application, but NOT the beneficiary. Chapter 3.

35. C. Your PIA determines your monthly income under Social Security. And your PIA is dependent on your average monthly income. Chapter 18.

36. C Naming the children on an irrevocable basis basically takes control of the policy away from the policyowner and gives it to the irrevocable beneficiary. Chapter 5.

37. D. There is a major difference between Interest Sensitive and Variable. Interest Sensitive guarantees a minimum rate. Variable means NO guaranteed rates of return. Chapters 4 & 7.

38. A. Group Life is a form of compensation and the premiums are deductible as an expense. Chapter 8.

© 2017 Pathfinder Corporation

LIFE FINAL EXAM ANSWER KEY

39.   D.   Mutual company dividends are not taxed because they are not income. Stockholder dividends are taxed as income. Chapter 1.

40.   C.   The cash values of life insurance policies or annuity contracts can NEVER be withdrawn from the policies tax free no matter what the age of the policyowner. Chapter 4.

41.   D.   The Guaranteed Insurability rider allows the policyowner to purchase more insurance on themselves from time to time but at the present attained age. Chapter 7.

42.   B.   Convertible term freezes your insurability, not your age. Choice C is incorrect because it is describing a feature of Interest Sensitive policies. Chapter 4.

43.   A.   The first two phrases in the question describe a Whole Life policy, but the third phrase describes a modified version of Whole Life called Graded Premium Whole Life. Chapter 7.

44.   D.   Under a Keogh plan, the employer must make an annual contribution to each eligible employee's plan equal to the same percentage as they make to their own account, in this case 10%. 10% of $25,000 is $2,500. Chapter 8.

45.   C.   The company will pay the face amount of the policy, $100,000, minus the outstanding loan of $5,000, for a payment of $95,000. Pays the death benefit or the cash value but not both. Chapter 4.

46.   D.   In the case of a policy surrender, the company will pay the cash value of $9,000 back to the policyowner minus the outstanding loan of $5,000, for a total of $4,000. Chapter 4.

47.   B.   If you make a collateral assignment, it is a temporary assignment. When you repay the loan, the assignment to the bank is cancelled, and all policy rights return to you. Chapter 5.

48.   D.   Third Party Ownership occurs when someone other than the insured owns the insurance policy, which is true in Group Life. Chapter 5.

49.   B.   Group Credit Life is used when borrowing money from a lending institution. The borrower's life is insured for the amount of the outstanding loan, and, unlike regular Group insurance, the beneficiary is the organizing entity of the group. Chapter 16.

LIFE FINAL EXAM ANSWER KEY

50.   C.   The NASD stands for the National Association of Securities Dealers. You must be licensed with them in order to sell securities (variable contracts). Chapter 4.

51.   B.   The Automatic Premium Loan provision begins if the policyowner has not paid the premium by the end of the grace period. Tim died within the grace period; the Automatic Premium Loan has not been triggered. Chapter 7.

52.   C.   Death during the grace period allows the company to subtract the overdue premium plus interest. Chapter 5.

53.   A.   Policy dividends can be taken in cash. The other option choices do not provide cash to the policyowner. Chapter 6.

54.   D.   By definition. Chapter 6.

55.   B.   Survivorship pays when the last one dies; Joint Life pays when the first one dies. Chapter 7.

56.   A.   Estate taxes are structured to impact the estate of a married couple at the death of the second person, thus Survivorship Life makes sense. Chapter 7.

57.   B.   By definition. See Chapter 4.

58.   D.   Misstatement of age means we just make it right. The insured had outlived the Suicide Clause restriction and the Incontestable Period. So none of these reasons are valid. Chapter 5.

59.   B.   Also known as The Right to Inspect the Policy. Chapter 5.

60.   C.   The Age 59 1/2 restriction only applies to annuities, qualified retirement plans and Modified Endowment Contracts, not to regular life policies. So a life policy can be surrendered for cash at any time, but the policyowner will have to pay the taxes on the growth. Chapter 4.

61.   B.   Re-Entry Term insurance is a form of Term that offers to give the policyowner a lower normal premium if the insured prove insurability at specified dates. Chapter 7.

62.   A.   The receipt of a policy dividend by the policyowner is simply the return of part of the premium because it was not needed by the company. Since this return is NOT income, it is not taxable. Chapter 1.

63. B. The Reduction Of Premium option is a Dividend option, not a Nonforfeiture option. Chapter 6.

64. B. All Variable contracts and mutual funds are security products and therefore require a securities license. Adjustable Life is not. Chapter 9.

65. B. By definition. Chapter 4.

66. A. The purpose of the Regulation is to allow a consumer to have adequate information regarding the relative cost of varying products. The Buyers Guide provides generic information. The Regulation does not cover group plans. The Regulation is silent as to medical exams.

67. C. A Producer must conduct a reasonable investigation regarding Replacement. The free look requirement in Replacement is 20 days. The Producer is required to notify his company, who then is required to notify the existing insurer. Under the Rule, the documents that are mentioned are the Important Notice Regarding Replacement of Life Insurance, and any sales proposals that are used.

68. C. The purpose of the Rule is not to prohibit or even limit Replacement, but rather make sure that the prospect has adequate information regarding the impact of replacing an existing policy.

69. D. Living Benefit Agreements do not provide any Disability income benefits. There are two types of Living Benefit Agreements, as explained on pages 1-40 through 1-43. This question refers to the Viatical Settlement contract, in which the Policyowner/Insured sells its policy to a third-party investor (Viatical) at a discount. Option C refers to Accellerated Death benefits, but ADB's do not pay 100% of the face value of the Life contract. Living wills have nothing to do with Living Benefit Agreements.

70. C. Replacement occurs when any value of an existing policy is significantly diminished. In A, the existing death benefit has been eliminated. In B, the cash value has been eliminated. Replacement includes borrowing more than 25% of the existing cash value (C).

71. D. A Temporary License is only issued when it is in the public interest, not the license holder's interest (A); Temporary Licensees may service existing accounts (B). The Temporary License does not require an examination (C). The license term is 180 days.

72. D. The limited lines license for Funeral Directors requires both prelicensing education and an examination.

73. C. The law requires that a Resident Producer <u>either</u> live in Indiana <u>or</u> have their primary place of business here.

© **2017 Pathfinder Corporation**

74.   B.   This is a rebate and is a violation of the law, and is never allowed. Controlled business is business that you write on yourself, your employer, your employees, your immediate family, or anything in which you have a significant interest.

75.   B.   The Commissioner has no set term, but rather serves at the pleasure of the Governor.

76.   D.   Because the President does not solicit, negotiate, or sell, no license is necessary.

77.   A.   An alien insurer is one that comes from outside the United States.

78.   C.   Hopefully all of your clients will be your friends.

79.   B.   30 days is the required limit, failure to do so is a violation of the Licensing Law.

80.   D.   The funeral director must pass the regular Life Insurance Producer's examination, even though a limited license will be issued.

81.   A.   Temporary Licenses are only issued in the public interest to service existing accounts under the 3-D Rule (Death, Disabled, Drafted).

82.   B.   While a Producer may, under certain circumstances, act like a Consultant, no person shall hold both licenses at the same time.

83.   A.   Offering to pay part of the premium is a rebate, and is forbidden. The gift of stock is also a rebate. Calling an insurance policy an investment is a violation of Rule 13. Charging varying rates to different classes is underwriting and is what make insurance economically feasible.

84.   D.   The Commissioner enforces the law (executive). The Commissioner may promulgate rules (legislative). The Commissioner may hold hearings and issue orders (judicial).

85.   A.   The Commissioner has the authority to examine all companies doing business in Indiana.

86.   B.   The amount of the bond is $50,000.

87.   D.   Any business entity may be licensed; only those employees acting as Producers must hold an individual license. The Compliance officer must be a licensed Producer.

LIFE FINAL EXAM ANSWER KEY

88. A. The Producer may act as a Consultant under these circumstances but may not hold a Consultant's license. C and D are illegal compensation arrangements.

89. C. There are not time limits in the Act. The only requirement is that things must be done in a reasonable manner.

90. B. The Policy Summary only covers information about a specific policy.

91. B. The company pays a discounted, reduced benefit based upon the prognosis of the viator.

92. D. The limitation on borrowing is 25%. The Producer has a duty to conduct a reasonable investigation. Replacement applies to both Term and Whole Life, and need only involve a single insurer.

93. D. The Conversion Period cannot be extended beyond 60 days.

94. C. Interest begins to accrue after 30 days.

95. D. The Death Benefit must be paid within two months of the receipt of proof of death.

96. C. This may be called a Viatical Settlement, simply a Viatical, or a Living Benefits Agreement. Accelerated Death Benefits are provided by the issuing insurer and not a third party.

97. B. The Commissioner promulgates rules to interpret the law. A rule has the same force and effect as the statute that it explains. The legislature passes statutes.

98. D. Interest begins to accrue 30 days after the submission of the valid proof of death, and is equal to the loan interest rate found in the policy.

99. C. The Viator is the insured and may be represented by a Viatical Broker. Viatical Producers represent the purchasing company. Consultants sell advice, and are not licensed to be involved in insurance transactions.

100. C. Cost is the difference between the money in and the money out.

HEALTH FINAL EXAM

1. In order to comply with the Fair Credit Reporting Act, an insurance producer is required to notify an applicant that a consumer credit report may be requested. The producer must notify the applicant about this at what point in time?

    (A) Before the end of the Ten Day Free Look period.
    (B) At the time of application for the policy.
    (C) When the insurance company actually requests the report.
    (D) Upon policy delivery.

2. Which of the following A&H coverages could provide reimbursement for medical expenses incurred as the result of a broken arm?

    (A) AD&D
    (B) LTC
    (C) Basic Hospital
    (D) Disability Income

3. The clause in a Disability Income Policy that outlines the coverages provided is the

    (A) Consideration clause.
    (B) Renewability clause.
    (C) Insuring clause.
    (D) Incontestable clause.

4. The universal requirement for eligibility for Medicaid is

    (A) Age 65 or over.
    (B) Permanent and total disability.
    (C) Dependent children.
    (D) Financial need.

5. In group A&H insurance, groups with high average age will usually have

    (A) Little or no exposure to disability income claims.
    (B) Above average maternity claims.
    (C) Above average claims.
    (D) Lower than average premiums.

© 2017 Pathfinder Corporation

6. Esther Olson recently purchased a two-year disability income policy. Her policy has a 10 day Elimination Period and a 30 day All-cause Probationary Period provision. If Esther is hospitalized for tuberculosis 15 days after her effective date of coverage, the maximum coverage available under her policy would be which of the following?

   (A) 2 years of benefits
   (B) 2 years minus 10 days of benefits
   (C) 2 years minus 30 days of benefits
   (D) No benefits will be paid.

7. Monte owns a long term disability income policy with a $1000 monthly benefit. His policy has a 30 day Elimination Period and 6 month Recurrent Disability Provision. Monte is totally disabled for 3 months. Eventually, he recuperates and returns to work. Two weeks after returning to work, Monte has a relapse and is again totally disabled, but for 5 months this time. What is the total amount of disability income benefits that Monte will collect?

   (A) $8,000
   (B) $7,000
   (C) $6,000
   (D) None of the above

8. Under the Uniform Individual Health Policy Provision Law, which of the following is true regarding the Grace Period Provision?

   (A) The premium mode determines the length of the Grace Period.
   (B) If the policyowner has a weekly premium mode, the grace period is 10 days.
   (C) Losses which occur during the Grace Period are not covered.
   (D) A grace period of 20 days is provided a policyowner who pays quarterly.

9. Little Red Riding Hood is covered by an AD&D policy from Big Bad Mutual. She is accosted by a wolf who bites her arm off at the elbow. Red submits a claim to Big Bad for the capital sum but is dismayed upon being notified by the insurer that according to company policy , losses due to wild animal bites are not covered. The provision in her policy which prevents Big Bad from referring to a company policy which was not contained in Red's contract is called the

   (A) Legal Actions Clause.
   (B) Time Limit on Certain Defenses Clause.
   (C) Entire Contract Changes Clause.
   (D) Insuring Clause.

© 2017 Pathfinder Corporation

HEALTH FINAL EXAM

10. Which of the following laws governs investigative consumer reports?

   (A) Freedom of Information Act
   (B) Consumer Protection Act
   (C) Fair Credit Reporting Act
   (D) NAIC Model Provisions

11. Mrs. Johnson has had a Major Medical policy with your company for five years and has filed numerous claims. She comes into your office and says that she is 45 days late in paying her premium and wants to pay you. You should do which of the following?

   (A) Assure her that the Automatic Premium Loan provision has kept her policy in force.
   (B) Take the money and waive the lapse.
   (C) Assure her that the grace period provision of her policy has kept her policy in force.
   (D) Take a reinstatement application.

Use the following numbers of days to answer questions 12 - 14. Each may be used once, more than once, or not at all.

   (A) 10 days
   (B) 20 days
   (C) 45 days
   (D) 60 days

12. The maximum number of days of back premium a company can collect with a reinstatement application on a Comprehensive Major Medical policy.

   (A)   (B)   (C)   (D)

13. The waiting period before coverage begins on sickness under a reinstated Major Medical policy.

   (A)   (B)   (C)   (D)

14. The number of days that an injured insured has to notify the insurance company of a loss?

   (A)   (B)   (C)   (D)

© 2017 Pathfinder Corporation

15. A Disability Income policy with a 90 day Elimination Period would

(A) Cost more than a policy with a 60 day Elimination Period.
(B) Waive the premium during the first 90 days of a covered disability income period.
(C) Pay benefits to be delivered to the insured on the 91st day of disability.
(D) Entitle the insured to become eligible for benefit payments starting on the 91st day of disability.

16. A Multiple Employer Welfare Arrangement (MEWA) or the Multiple Employer Trust (MET) have all of the following characteristics EXCEPT

(A) They are usually acceptable for Group insurance under state law.
(B) They are designed to provide medical expense benefits to their members.
(C) They are a form of social assistance program mandated by Title 19 of the Social Security Act.
(D) They traditionally were used for groups that were too small to qualify for true Group insurance.

17. Which of the following statements is true about the taxation of premium and proceeds of health insurance contracts?

(A) Group noncontributory Disability Income policy benefits payable to employees are taxable as ordinary income.
(B) Group noncontributory medical expense benefits payable to employees are taxable as ordinary income.
(C) Individually purchased Disability Income policy benefits are taxable as ordinary income.
(D) Individually purchased Medical Expenses policy benefits are taxable as ordinary income.

18. OASDI is commonly referred to as which of the following?

(A) Social Security benefits
(B) Workers Compensation
(C) Center for Medicare and Medicaid Services
(D) Internal Revenue Service

19. Assume that you are insured by a individual Major Medical policy written through an HMO. If you have a loss, the policy would require you to do all of the following EXCEPT:

(A) Use approved providers for non-emergency treatment.
(B) Submit to a medical exam if requested by the insurer.
(C) Pay the provider in advance and then submit a claim for reimbursement to the insurer.
(D) Visit your Primary Care Physician prior to seeing a specialist in a non-emergency situation.

20. Bill Blake worked as a window washer at a high rise office building when he purchased a Disability Income policy with a $500 weekly benefit. He quit his job six months ago and became a librarian, without notifying his company. He will receive which of the following amounts if he becomes disabled?

(A) more than $500 per week.
(B) less than $500 per week.
(C) $500 per week.
(D) $500 per week and a refund of the unearned premium collected.

21. Helen has a Major Medical policy with a $500 deductible, an 80%/20% coinsurance clause and a stop loss feature of $10,000. She suffers a heart attack while driving, and the subsequent accident requires the amputation of an arm. Medical bills total $9,500. She further is considered to be permanently partially disabled and suffers a 20% loss of her $50,000 a year income. Helen's Major Medical policy will pay which of the following?

(A) $ 2,300
(B) $ 7,200
(C) $ 7,700
(D) $17,200

22. Which of the following activities would NOT be part of a managed care health care system?

(A) Utilization Review
(B) Second Opinion
(C) Elective cosmetic surgery
(D) Preventive Care

23. Chevy Chase is making a good living as a comedian but he is concerned that if he were to become permanently partially disabled, he could lose a substantial amount of his income for the rest of his earning years. Which of the following coverages could resolve Chevy's concerns?

(A) Partial Disability
(B) Residual Disability
(C) Total Disability
(D) None of the above

24. Paula McGee has a Disability Income policy which has a $1,000 monthly benefit. On the second month of a covered disability, she receives her first check for $875 and each subsequent check is also for $875. When she asks the reason for this, the most likely rationale is that the company applied which of the following?

(A) A Deductible
(B) An Elimination Period
(C) A Probationary Period
(D) The Change of Occupation Provision

25. Brock Lee Spears is a Certified Public Accountant (CPA). He owns a small firm in which he is the primary income producer. He also has an accounting assistant and a secretary. Which of the following policies would you recommend to Brock in order to cover his business expenses?

(A) Key Employee Disability Income Policy
(B) Business Disability Buy Out
(C) Business Overhead Expense
(D) SSDI

26. All of the following clauses can be used by an insurance company to screen out preexisting conditions EXCEPT the

(A) Insuring Clause.
(B) Probationary Period.
(C) Elimination Period.
(D) Impairment Rider.

© 2017 Pathfinder Corporation

HEALTH FINAL EXAM

27. Two weeks ago, you took an application from Cary Grant for a Major Medical policy to cover his family. No premium was paid in advance. You have just received the policy from your company. Why would it be very important for you to deliver this policy to Cary as soon as possible?

    (A) Because the insurance company needs the money.
    (B) Because you are personally liable for Cary's health risks from the date of application.
    (C) There will be no coverage in force until you deliver the policy and collect the initial premium,
    (D) There is no need to hurry as the coverage has been in effect since the date of application.

28. Which of the following government programs is public assistance?

    (A) Medicare Part A and Part B
    (B) Medicaid
    (C) COBRA
    (D) Social Security Disability Income

29. All of the following health coverages might make use of an elimination or waiting period EXCEPT

    (A) Business Disability Buy Out.
    (B) Business Overhead Expense.
    (C) Key Employee Disability Income.
    (D) Medicare Parts A & B.

30. Flora and Fauna are identical twins. Five years ago, each purchased individual Disability Income policies with the same dollar benefits. Though they both work as secretaries for the same company, Flora's premium is 50% higher than Fauna's. This difference could be due to all of the following EXCEPT

    (A) The insuring clauses differ.
    (B) The elimination periods differ.
    (C) The definition sections differ.
    (D) The dependent children coverages differ.

HEALTH FINAL EXAM

31. Most life and health insurance policies are written by the insurance company and are offered to the applicant on a take it or leave it basis. Such contracts are referred to as

   (A) Conditional.
   (B) Unilateral.
   (C) Contract of Adhesion.
   (D) Executory.

32. Zip McClain has a Medical Expense policy with a $1,000 Base plan, a $200 deductible, and an 80%/20% coinsurance clause. He is admitted to the hospital with a covered illness. His bill totals $9,200. His policy will pay which of the following?

   (A) $6,400
   (B) $7,200
   (C) $7,400
   (D) None of the above.

33. Which of the following Uniform Policy Provisions does NOT state a time to complete certain actions in the claims handling process?

   (A) Claim Forms
   (B) Payment of Claims
   (C) Time of Payment of Claims
   (D) Proof of Loss

34. Four years ago Julie purchased a Disability Income policy. If she files a claim today and the insurer now discovers that Julie is 5 years older than she stated on the application, the insurer will probably do which of the following?

   (A) Pay the claim, as the incontestable period has expired.
   (B) Deny the claim based on a material misrepresentation on the application.
   (C) Adjust the benefits downward based on what Julie's premium would have purchased in coverage based on her correct age.
   (D) Pay an amount higher that the benefit stated in the policy.

35. Lynn Wilson purchases a Medical Expense policy with a $1,000 Base plan, a $200 deductible, and an 80%/20% coinsurance clause. She is hospitalized for a covered illness, and the bills total $5,200. She anticipates that her company will pay $4,200, but it only pays $3,752. All of the following characteristics of a Medical Expense policy could account for this discrepancy on Lynn's first claim EXCEPT

   (A) Customary, Reasonable and Necessary Expenses provision.
   (B) Policy exclusions.
   (C) The elimination period.
   (D) Inside limits.

36. Which of the following is true regarding Blue Cross/Blue Shield?

   (A) The participants in a Blue Cross/Blue Shield plan are called subscribers.
   (B) Blue Cross is a service organization which provides medical and surgical benefits; Blue Shield provides hospitalization benefits.
   (C) Blue Cross/Blue Shield is a corporation organized on a national basis.
   (D) In most of the country, Blue Cross/Blue Shield operates on a for profit basis.

37. Which of the following health provisions would permit a policyowner to NOT pay the premium during a period of disability?

   (A) Payor Benefit
   (B) Residual Disability
   (C) Waiver of Premium
   (D) Recurrent Disability

38. All of the following could be secondary payors under Medicare EXCEPT:

   (A) SSDI
   (B) Medicaid
   (C) MSP
   (D) Individuals

39.   Which of the following is true of an Impairment Rider?

(A)   It makes obtaining insurance possible for an otherwise uninsurable person.
(B)   It can be purchased as a stand-alone policy.
(C)   It applies to all insureds covered under the policy without discrimination.
(D)   It provides coverage for impairments which would normally be excluded as preexisting conditions.

40.   Midwest Mutual receives a prepaid application for a Major Medical policy from Ivella Ketousky. Seven days later, Midwest Mutual receives the MIB report on Ivella which shows that she suffered a recent heart attack that was not disclosed on the application. The company may take all of the following actions EXCEPT:

(A)   Tell the producer that Ivella will not be insured.
(B)   Have the MIB tell Ivella why she will be denied coverage.
(C)   Return Ivella's premium to her.
(D)   Deny Ivella's application for coverage.

41.   Which of the following is true concerning waiver of premium in Disability Income policies?

(A)   If the insured policyowner becomes disabled, the insurance company will waive the premium for the rest of the life of the contract.
(B)   If the insured becomes permanently partially disabled, the insurance company will waive the premium for the remainder of the life of the contract.
(C)   If the insured policyowner becomes totally disabled, the insurance company will waive the premium payments for the duration of the disability after a stated period of time, such as 90 days.
(D)   If the insured dies, the insurance company will waive the premium on the insured's dependent children until the dependent children reach the age of majority.

42. As an employee of XYZ Corporation, you are a member of their noncontributory Group health insurance program. You have just been laid off. The really bad news is that you suffer from an ongoing heart problem. Which of the following is true concerning your XYZ benefits?

    (A) Under COBRA you may stay in the XYZ plan for a limited period of time.
    (B) You are probably eligible for SSDI.
    (C) HIPAA allows you to convert to an individual policy of health insurance because proof of insurability is not required.
    (D) You will be entitled to Accelerated Death Benefits but not to COBRA.

43. Which of the following health riders would NOT increase the premium?

    (A) Guaranteed Insurability
    (B) Future Income Option
    (C) Multiple Indemnity
    (D) Impairment

44. A type of health contract which would provide the funds necessary for the remaining healthy partners in a business to purchase the interest of a disabled business partner is called

    (A) Key Employee/Person Health.
    (B) Business Overhead Expense.
    (C) Business Disability Buy-Out.
    (D) Business Interruption.

45. Which of the following health care providers traditionally provides services to its members at its own local health care facilities?

    (A) HMO
    (B) PPO
    (C) MEWA
    (D) MET

46.   Jacob is a member of a Group Major Medical plan at work. The plan is non-contributory and it is underwritten by ABC Insurance Company. Jacob's wife, Mary, also works and is covered by a Group Major Medical plan at her place of employment which is underwritten by XYZ Company. Both plans have Nonduplication and Coordination of Benefits Clauses and cover both spouses. Jacob is injured in a covered accident. Covered medical costs total $5,500. Both policies have a $500 deductible and an 80/20 coinsurance clause. Which of the following insurance carriers would be secondary/excess and how much would it pay?

(A)   ABC is secondary and would pay $4,000
(B)   XYZ is secondary and would pay $4,000
(C)   ABC is secondary and would pay $1,500
(D)   XYZ is secondary and would pay $1,500

47.   Today, most individuals purchasing Long-Term Care policies are

(A)   Young families who need catastrophic medical expense coverages.
(B)   Middle income families wishing to protect their income against loss of income from a long-term disability.
(C)   Businesses desiring to insure their key employees against prolonged illnesses.
(D)   Middle income, middle aged individuals wishing to provide for the day when they can no longer live without some type of assistance.

48.   All of the following are characteristics of group insurance EXCEPT:

(A)   Reduced adverse selection
(B)   Medical exams are always required
(C)   Group underwriting
(D)   Lower commission rates

49.   All of the following are true regarding Group Disability Income insurance EXCEPT:

(A)   The coverage may be provided under either a contributory or a noncontributory plan.
(B)   It may cover both occupational and nonoccupational losses.
(C)   The benefits may be coordinated with SSDI benefits and Workers Compensation benefits.
(D)   Group DI policies may be converted to individual policies at the termination of employment under COBRA

© 2017 Pathfinder Corporation

50. COBRA

 (A) Provides for a continuation of health coverages for physically or mentallly handicapped dependent children.
 (B) Offers the continuation of health coverages for departing employees.
 (C) Guarantees the solvency of insurance companies facing financial difficulty.
 (D) Provides health coverages for economically needy households.

51. Mr. Methuselah is so old that he needs help in dressing, getting in and out of bed and feeding himself. His Long Term Care policy will provide which of the following benefits?

 (A) Convalescent care
 (B) Custodial care
 (C) Recuperative care
 (D) Residual care

52. The insurance company's consideration is found in the

 (A) Reinstatement clause.
 (B) Insuring clause.
 (C) Incontestable clause.
 (D) Tiger clause.

53. Which of the following is **NOT** true in most states concerning the rights of dependent children?

 (A) Healthy dependent children who continue to live at home with their parents after the completion of college must be covered by the insurance company as long as the parents continue to pay the proper premium.
 (B) Newly adopted children are normally covered by Major Medical policies on the date of placement without proof of insurability.
 (C) Medical Expense coverage for newborn children starts at the moment of birth.
 (D) Mentally handicapped children who continue to chiefly depend upon their parents for support and maintenance can continue coverage under their parents policy with continued proof of eligibility.

54. Under a Disability Income Policy, which of the following definitions of total disability would be the most expensive to purchase?

(A) Any Occupation
(B) Own Occupation, Then Any Occupation
(C) Own Occupation
(D) Presumptive Total Disability

55. According to the NAIC model legislation, all the following are characteristics of Long-Term Care policies EXCEPT

(A) Benefits must be provided for not less than 12 consecutive months.
(B) Renewability must be written on either a Guaranteed Renewable or Noncancellable basis.
(C) Preexisting conditions may be excluded from coverage for up to two years after the policy date.
(D) An Outline of Coverages must be provided to prospective applicants before the initial premium is collected.

Use the following to answer questions 56-58. Each may be used once, more than once, or not at all.

(A) Noncancellable
(B) Period of Time
(C) Conditionally Renewable
(D) Guaranteed Renewable

56. The minimum level of renewability that can be offered in a Medicare Supplement Policy sold today.

(A)   (B)   (C)   (D)

57. The best level of renewability that could be offered.

(A)   (B)   (C)   (D)

58. The form of renewal granted in Flight Insurance policies.

(A)   (B)   (C)   (D)

© 2017 Pathfinder Corporation

HEALTH FINAL EXAM

59.   All of the following are considered ADLs EXCEPT:

(A)   Eating
(B)   Bathing
(C)   Mobility
(D)   Smoking

60.   All of the following are true regarding the right to return a health insurance policy in Indiana EXCEPT

(A)   All Medicare Supplement Policies are required to have a 30 Day Free Look.
(B)   Health insurance policies generally require at least a 10 Day Free Look.
(C)   The inspection period begins on the effective date of coverage.
(D)   A claim paid during the Free Look period will negate the right to return.

61.   The purpose of the Medicare Supplement Policy law is to do all of the following EXCEPT

(A)   Standardize the coverages contained in MSPs.
(B)   Simplify the terms and benefits of MSPs.
(C)   Eliminate provisions which mislead or confuse the public in connection with MSPs.
(D)   Mandate that all MSP policies issued contain the same coverage.

62.   Under Indiana law, a health insurance company which issues individual medical expense policies must do all of the following EXCEPT

(A)   Continue coverage beyond age 19 for handicapped dependents who are incapable of self-sustaining employment and chiefly dependent upon the policyowner for support and maintenance.
(B)   Automatically cover newborn children from the moment of birth as long as the policyowner notifies the insurance company within 31 days of the birth and pays additional premium if required.
(C)   Cover a newly adopted child from the date of placement.
(D)   Accept a mentally or physically handicapped foster child.

© 2017 Pathfinder Corporation

63. An advertisement under Indiana insurance law would include which of the following?

    (A)   Classified advertisements designed to recruit producers.
    (B)   Scripts for memorized oral sales presentations.
    (C)   A company newsletter to its employees and stockholders.
    (D)   None of the above.

64. LTC policies will NOT pay benefits for

    (A)   Home health care.
    (B)   Acute hospital care.
    (C)   Nursing home care.
    (D)   Residential care.

65. If you are a 40 year old resident of Indiana, uninsurable but not broke, you can best obtain coverages through which of the following?

    (A)   Indiana Comprehensive Health Insurance Plan
    (B)   Medicaid
    (C)   COBRA
    (D)   Medicare

66. If your Producer's license is revoked, you must do which of the following?

    (A)   Destroy the license.
    (B)   Return your license to your agency manager.
    (C)   Return your license to your employing company.
    (D)   Return your license to the Commissioner, either in person or by mail.

67. The penalty assessed by the Commissioner for a producer who is less than 12 months late in renewing their license:

    (A)   Is an additional 8 hours of continuing education or a $500 fine.
    (B)   Is the retaking of the state law portion of the licensing examination.
    (C)   Is twice the renewal fee.
    (D)   May be waived if the lapse is less than 30 days.

68. The Insurance Commissioner may revoke or deny your Producer's license if you do any of the following EXCEPT

    (A)   Write controlled business.
    (B)   Cheat on your licensing exam.
    (C)   Forge another's name on an insurance application.
    (D)   Misrepresent the terms of a policy.

69. The Commissioner must do which of the following to all authorized insurers on a regular basis?

    (A)   Rehabilitate
    (B)   Consolidate
    (C)   Liquidate
    (D)   Examine

70. Which of the following persons must have an insurance license?

    (A)   The president of an insurance company.
    (B)   An agency secretary who calculates insurance rates.
    (C)   An attorney who charges a fee for insurance advice.
    (D)   A person soliciting baggage insurance in a transportation terminal.

71. The Indiana Unfair Claims Settlement Practices law states that the company must acknowledge your claim within how long?

    (A)   10 days
    (B)   15 days
    (C)   30 days
    (D)   A reasonable period

72. A producer's license must be renewed:

    (A)   Every six months.
    (B)   Every year.
    (C)   Every two years.
    (D)   Every four years.

73. The Commissioner of Insurance can do all of the following to a Producer engaged in dishonest practices EXCEPT

    (A)   Censure a producer.
    (B)   Suspend the producer's license.
    (C)   Fine the producer.
    (D)   Put the producer in jail.

74. Under Indiana law, which of the following is NOT true about the Indiana Comprehensive Health Insurance Plan?

    (A)   It is designed to provide protection for those who cannot economically buy through normal channels.
    (B)   The Pre-existing Conditions clause will be waived if the insured had coverage under another medical expense plan within the last 6 months.
    (C)   Insureds cannot be charged more than standard rates.
    (D)   All Health insurers doing business in Indiana must belong to the plan.

75. Long Term Care Insurance Policy means either an individual policy or a Group policy that provides coverage in a nursing home or other similar health care facility for at least how many consecutive months?

    (A)   6 months
    (B)   12 months
    (C)   24 months
    (D)   36 months

76. A Medicare Supplement policy can exclude coverage for preexisting conditions for up to how many months?

    (A)   6
    (B)   12
    (C)   24
    (D)   None of the above

77. All of the following are true regarding Medicare Supplement insurance marketed in Indiana EXCEPT

    (A) MSP policies cannot be written as a service plan

    (B) The insurance company must provide the applicant with an outline of the proposed MSP.

    (C) As a Producer, you are required to provide your customer with a signed receipt for all materials you received during the solicitation in addition to giving them your name, office address and phone number.

    (D) An MSP must contain a 30 Day Free Look provision.

78. The mandatory Outline of Coverages for a Long Term Care policy must include all of the following EXCEPT

    (A) A description of the benefits.

    (B) An explanation of the renewal provisions.

    (C) A 10 Day Free Look provision.

    (D) A description of the major exclusions.

79. Which of the following types of coverages would NOT be provided by an LTC policy?

    (A) Home health care

    (B) Intermediate care

    (C) Acute hospital care

    (D) Nursing home care

80. All of the following would be part of an MSP policy EXCEPT

    (A) 30 Day Free Look.

    (B) Rights of Renewability.

    (C) Definition of terms.

    (D) Supplementary Medical insurance.

81. All of the following impact group A&H coverages EXCEPT

    (A) Indiana Small Group Statute.

    (B) HIPAA.

    (C) Rule 38.1. (Coordination of Benefits)

    (D) ICHIA.

82. The premium for coverage under the Indiana Comprehensive Health Insurance Association is determined by

   (A)   Normal underwriting criteria.
   (B)   The Commissioner.
   (C)   The average premium charged by the state's largest insurers.
   (D)   The CPI.

83. The Indiana LTCP

   (A)   Virtually eliminates the need for Medicaid.
   (B)   Splits nursing home costs with Medicare.
   (C)   Provides an incentive for purchasing LTC coverage.
   (D)   Is funded by the Federal government.

84. Under Rule 38.1, the primary coverage for the children of a divorced couple is

   (A)   Coverage obtained through ICHIA.
   (B)   The coverage of the custodial parent.
   (C)   The coverage of the parent who is the subject of a child support order.
   (D)   The coverage of the parent whose birthday falls first during the calendar year.

85. Under the Indiana Small Group Statute, insurance companies

   (A)   Are restricted in their ability to cancel or nonrenew coverages.
   (B)   Must issue coverage to all employees from the first day of employment.
   (C)   Must charge all groups the same premium per member.
   (D)   Must all offer coverage for small groups.

86. ADL's are

   (A)   Accrued Disability Limits.
   (B)   Accelerated Death Liabilities.
   (C)   Activities of Daily Living.
   (D)   Anti-Discrimination Levels.

© 2017 Pathfinder Corporation

87. The Indiana Small Group Statute operates

   (A)   In coordination with HIPAA.
   (B)   In place of HIPAA.
   (C)   In coordination with ICHIA.
   (D)   In coordination with the ILTCP.

88. Under Indiana Law, a pro rata return of unearned premium shall be made

   (A)   Should the insured die prior to filing a claim under an LTC policy.
   (B)   Should a claim already have been paid on a policy which is being returned under a free look provision.
   (C)   Should the insured die during the policy period on a medical expense policy.
   (D)   Should the company deny claim based upon a pre-existing condition.

89. Under Indiana Law, all of the following are required provisions in A&H policies EXCEPT the

   (A)   Entire Contract Clause.
   (B)   Incontestable Clause.
   (C)   Relation To Earnings Clause.
   (D)   Suicide Clause.

90. ICHIA is organized as

   (A)   A division of the Department of Insurance.
   (B)   A supplement to Medicaid.
   (C)   A supplement to Medicare.
   (D)   A pool of all companies writing A&H coverage.

91. Under ICHIA a pre-existing conditions exclusion pertains to a medical condition that has occurred in the last:

   (A)   Month.
   (B)   3 months.
   (C)   180 days.
   (D)   Year.

HEALTH FINAL EXAM

92. According to Indiana health insurance law, a base line mammogram photo must be offered to every woman who is at least:

    (A) 21 years of age.
    (B) 25 years of age.
    (C) 30 years of age.
    (D) 35 years of age.

93. The premium charged for a health insurance policy converted from a small group health plan would be limited to:

    (A) 50 percent of the group premium.
    (B) 75 percent of the group premium.
    (C) 100 percent of the group premium.
    (D) 150 percent of the group premium.

END

EXAM ANSWERS & EXPLANATIONS ON NEXT PAGE

© 2017 Pathfinder Corporation

HEALTH FINAL EXAM
ANSWER KEY

1. B. The Fair Credit Reporting Act requires that an applicant be informed at the time of application. Chapter 3.

2. C. A Basic Hospital policy is a medical expense policy and therefore would pay for the medical expenses incurred for a broken arm. AD&D would pay for the loss of an arm but not for the medical expenses to fix an arm. Chapters 12 & 14

3. C. No matter what type of insurance you are examining, the insurance company's promises/coverages are contained in the Insuring Clause. Chapter 5.

4. D. Medicaid is a welfare program, not an insurance program. As such, to be eligible you must be broke plus have one other hardship situation, such as to be over age 65 or to be permanently and totally disabled. Chapter 18.

5. C. A group with a high average age is, therefore, higher than average risk. The result will usually be above average claims. Chapter 16.

6. D. Esther's policy contains a 30 day Probationary Period. Therefore, any loss suffered within 30 days after the policy effective date will not be covered. Chapter 10.

7. B. Monte's monthly income benefit is $1000. However, he will not be paid for the first 30 days of any loss period because the policy contains a 30 day Elimination Period. But, according to his Recurrent Disability Provision, if Monte suffers a relapse during the next six months, he would not be charged a second 30 day time deductible. Therefore, Monte was disabled for eight months and would be charged only one deductible, for a total income of $7,000. Chapter 11.

8. A. Unlike life insurance policies, health insurance policy Grace Periods are determined by your premium mode: 7, 10, 31, Weekly, Monthly, All Other. Chapter 15.

9. C. The Entire Contract clause says that info which is not in the policy or the app doesn't count. Company Policy is irrelevant. Chapter 15.

10. C.   Investigative Consumer Reports are regulated by the Fair Credit Reporting Act. Chapter 3.

11. D.   Unlike cash value Life insurance policies, health insurance policies do not have cash values to sustain them beyond the Grace Period. So at the end of the Grace Period, health policies lapse. And the Company has no obligation to reinstate them. But they may. The process is to take a reinstatement application, collect up to 60 days of past due premium and issue a conditional receipt. Even after all of that, the company still has the right not to reinstate the policyowner if they think the risk is too great. Chapter 15.

12. D.   60 days back premium. Chapter 15.

13. A.   10 day probationary period. Chapter 15.

14. B.   20 days for notice. Chapter 15.

15. D.   A Disability Income policy with a 90 day Elimination Period will NOT even start earning DI benefits for the policyowner until the 91st day of the loss. If benefits were to be paid monthly, it would be on the 120th day of the loss before the first check would be mailed. Chapter 11.

16. C.   C is just flat incorrect. METs and MEWAs are not government aid programs. Chapter 16.

17. A.   This may help: Medical expense benefits paid for you from any source Auto, Uncle Sam, VA, medical expense policies whatever are never taxed. Disability Income benefits are different. If you buy a DI policy for yourself, you pay the premium with after tax dollars. Therefore, any income benefits received will not be taxed. Noncontributory Group DI benefits, however, are purchased with before tax dollars, and therefore all benefits paid are taxed as ordinary income. Chapter 10.

18. A.   OASDI = Social Security. Chapter 18.

19. C.   Since the HMO is both the insurance company and the health care provider, there is no need for the insured to pay for services or submit claims. Chapter 10.

20. D.   In this situation, Bill has gone from a high risk occupation to a low risk occupation without informing the insurance company. Therefore, according to the Change Of Occupation provision, the company will pay the $500 per week benefit and refund the unearned premium. Chapter 15.

21. B.   Helen's medical expense loss = $9,500. First subtract the $500 deductible that Helen must pay. That leaves $9,000. Then the company will pay 80% of the $9,000 = $7,200. A Major Medical policy will not pay any benefits for lost income. Chapter 12.

22. C.   Managed Care is all about saving money on health care. Obviously elective cosmetic surgery is not about saving money. Chapter 10.

23. B.   The Disability Income benefit that is designed to pay long term partial disability income benefits is called the Residual Disability Income Benefit, not the Partial Disability Benefit. Chapter 11.

24. D.   This is a very difficult question! About the only way you can answer it is by the process of elimination. The fact that Paula did not receive any income during the first month is explainable by choice A a deductible. In a DI contract, the deductible is a time deductible, not a dollar deductible, and is called an Elimination Period. So B is essentially the same as A. C, the Probationary Period, starts on the policy effective date and has nothing to do with the claim process. So that leaves you with D by default. D is correct. If Paula had changed from a lower risk occupation to a higher risk occupation, and then had a loss, she would in fact receive less than her stated monthly benefit. Chapter 15.

25. C.   The Business Overhead Expense policy is designed for small businesses that are dependent on the earning ability of the owner to pay the bills. If this breadwinner becomes disabled, then the business itself is in jeopardy. The BOE policy is a type of DI contract that pays the normal operating business expenses should the key income producer become disabled. Chapter 11.

26. C.   The Elimination Period is a deductible. Deductibles have nothing to do with protecting the company against preexisting conditions. Chapter 11.

27. C.   If there is no premium sent in to the company with the application, then the Producer must deliver the policy to the proposed insured in order to collect the premium. No money, no coverage! Chapter 2.

28. B.   Medicaid is a welfare/public assistance program, not an insurance program. Chapter 18.

29. D.   Elimination Periods only occur in Disability Income policies; A, B and C are DI policies. Chapter 11.

© 2017 PATHFINDER Corporation

30. D. A, B and C could have an impact on what premium is charged. But D could not, because the Rights Of Dependent Children only appear in medical expense policies, and this question is about Disability Income policies. Chapter 12.

31. C. Contracts Of Adhesion = one author. Chapter 2.

32. C. Zip owns a Comprehensive Major Medical policy. Therefore, Zip's Base Plan will pay the first $1,000 in benefits. Then Zip would pay his $200 deductible. So start with the loss of $9,200, subtract the $1,000 and the $200 = $8,000. Now the Major Medical portion of the policy will pay 80% of $8,000 = $6,400. Add the $1,000 paid by the base plan to the $6,400 = $7,400 paid by the company. Chapter 12.

33. B. The Payment Of Claims provision states to whom benefits are paid, not when the benefits must be paid. Chapter 15.

34. C. This question is about the Misstatement Of Age provision, which states that if the Insured has misstated their age, the insurance company will adjust the benefits. Chapter 15.

35. C. The Elimination Period only appears in Disability Income policies, not Medical Expense policies. This question is about Medical Expense coverages. Chapter 11.

36. A. Most Blue Cross/Blue Shield organizations refer to their policyowners/ insureds as Subscribers. Chapter 10.

37. C. The Waiver Of Premium provision found in Disability Income policies allows a disabled insured to not pay the premium during a period of disability. It is a temporary waiver. Chapter 11.

38. A. Medicare is a medical expense policy. SSDI is Social Security Disability Income. No DI policy would be a Secondary Payor to a medical expense policy. Chapter 13 & 18.

39. A. A person whose hobby is bungee jumping might be uninsurable. An Impairment Rider could exclude injuries attributable to that hobby this making the person insurable. Chapter 10.

40. B. Ivella is guilty of material misrepresentation because she failed to tell the insurance company of her recent heart attack. But it is the company's responsibility to tell Ivella, not the MIB's. Chapters 2 & 3.

© 2017 Pathfinder Corporation

41. C. The Waiver Of Premium benefit in DI policies is only triggered by Total Disability, not Partial Disability or Death. And it is a temporary waiver, not permanent. There is also a waiting period, such as 90 days. Chapter 11.

42. A. COBRA has you covered . You have been laid off, which is one of the many triggers for COBRA. And because you have a serious preexisting heart condition, you really need to stay under the XYZ group plan for as long as possible (up to eighteen months) or until you find work with a new employer and become fully eligible for their health plan. Chapter 17.

43. D. Riders that add coverages or benefits increase the premium. However, the Impairment Rider does not increase benefits. It actually eliminates benefits for a specific ailment or activity.Chapter 10.

44. C. Buy-Sell Agreements allow the surviving partner in a small business to buy the other half of the business from the deceased partner. The companion policy that does essentially the same thing if a partner becomes disabled and can no longer work is called Business Disability Buy-Out. Chapter 11.

45. A. HMOs traditionally provided both the insurance and the health care services at their own clinics/hospitals. PPOs typically sub-contract the health care services to other providers. Chapter 10.

46. D. Primary Coverage goes with the injured Insured. Since Jacob is the injured Insured, his coverage, ABC, is Primary for this loss. Under the Coordination Of Benefits clause, the Primary Insured will pay as if there were no other insurance involved. And then the Secondary Insurer must waive its own deductible and co-payments and pay all that the Primary Insurer won't pay. The loss was $5,500. Subtract the $500 deductible = $5,000. Take 80% of $5,000 = $4,000. So the Primary Insurer will pay $4,000. This means that the Secondary must pay the balance = $1,500. Chapter 17.

47. D. Long Term Care is usually considered to be a coverage most appropriate for Senior Citizens. However, middle aged folks planning for their future should be purchasing LTC while the rates are more favorable. Chapter 13.

48. B. Medical exams are rarely required in large group plans. Chapter 16.

49. D. COBRA (and even HIPAA) regulates the continuance of Medical Expense coverages, not Disability Income coverages. Chapter 17.

50. B. COBRA offers the continuance of Group medical expense coverages for departing employees. Chapter 17

51. B. What Mr. Methuselah needs help doing, such as feeding himself or getting in or out of bed, are referred to as Activities Of Daily Living ADLs which are treated by Custodial Care. Chapter 13.

52. B. What the insurance company gives to the policyowner of value, which is called consideration, are the promises to pay benefits in the future. These promises are contained in the Insuring Clause. Chapters 2 & 5.

53. A. Healthy dependents who are over 19 and no longer students cannot continue under a parent's plan. Chapter 12.

54. C. The best definition of Total Disability under a DI contract is the Own Occupation definition, and, therefore, the most expensive. Chapter 11.

55. C. The NAIC model legislation for LTC policies calls for a six month limit for the preexisting conditions exclusion. Chapter 13.

56. D. MSPs require one of the two highest forms of Renewability. Chapter 13.

57. A. The highest form of Renewability is Noncancellable. Chapter 10.

58. B. Flight Insurance policies cannot be renewed. If you need more coverage, you must purchase a new policy. Chapter 10.

59. D. ADL's Activities Of Daily Living necessary activities do not include smoking. Chapter 13.

Questions 60 - 93 are on Indiana State Law.

60. C. The Free Look begins on the delivery date (you can't look at it unless you've got it) and this may not be the same as the delivery date.

61. D. Not all MSP policies offer the same coverages. There are ten approved forms, Forms A-J.

62. D. The Handicapped and Dependent Child provision merely restricts the situations in which a company can remove a handicapped dependent child from coverage upon reaching the terminating age; the provision does not require that insurers accept handicapped children.

63. B. An advertisement is any attempt to communicate with consumers.

© 2017 Pathfinder Corporation

HEALTH FINAL EXAM ANSWER KEY

64. B. Acute care is treatment and is better covered elsewhere.

65. A. The Indiana Comprehensive Health Insurance Association (ICHIA) is the pool that provides affordable coverage for those who cannot find it, at a feasible rate on the open market.

66. D. The license is deemed to be the property of the state and must, upon revocation, be returned to the Commissioner.

67. D. The penalty in this situation would be 3 times the renewal fees, and be waived if the application is less than 30 days late.

68. A. Controlled business is limited to 25% of commission income, but is not prohibited.

69   D. The Commissioner is required to examine all admitted companies at least every 5 years (in the case of a foreign or alien insurer, where the home state complies with the NAIC examination procedures, the Commissioner may waive the Indiana examination).

70. D. The person selling baggage insurance would need a limited license. **NOTE:** the agency secretary can calculate rates all day long without a license, as long as she does not communicate them to consumers.

71. D. There are no specific time lines in the statute; the only requirement is that all actions be reasonable.

72. C. A Producer's license must be renewed every two years

73. D. Only judges can jail individuals.

74. C. ICHIA insureds can be charged 150% of the standard rate of the state's 5 largest insurers.

75. B. Twelve consecutive months of benefits is the minimum.

76. A. Six months is the maximum.

77. A. Indiana law allows, and the federal government encourages, service MSP plans.

78. C. The Free Look for Long Term Care policies is 30 days.

79. C. Acute care is treatment and is better covered elsewhere.

© 2017 Pathfinder Corporation

HEALTH FINAL EXAM ANSWER KEY

80.　D.　Supplementary Medical Coverage is not part of an MSP, it is actually the proper name for Medicare Part B.

81.　D.　ICHIA is a pool that issues individual coverages for uninsurable persons. Rule 38.1 is the Coordination of Benefits Rule. HIPAA is the federal statue that governs the underwriting and portability of group health. The Small Group Statute governs group health plans of between 2 and 50 persons in Indiana.

82.　C.　More specifically, it is the standard premium charged by the five largest insurers.

83.　C.　The incentive being the ability to shelter wealth from the ravages of the Medicaid spend down.

84.　C.　The first birthday rule does not apply in the case of divorce. The plan of the parent who is the subject of the child support order is the primary coverage.

85.　A.　The statute regulates the continuation of small group coverage. The statute does allow for probationary periods (B); experience rating (C) and allows companies to opt out of the small group business in its entirety (D).

86.　C.　ADL's are activities of daily living. There are five of them: bathing, eating, dressing, getting in and out of bed, getting around.

87.　A.　Indiana law does not trump federal law, HIPAA, but coordinates with it.

88.　C.　The insured will not accrue any further medical expenses, therefore the unearned premium must be returned.

89.　D.　The Suicide Clause is a Life insurance provision, and in fact A&H policies with a death benefit (AD&D) can, and often do, exclude suicide. The Relation to Earnings Clause is optional under the NAIC model provisions, but it is mandatory in Indiana.

90.　D.　ICHIA is a pool.

91.　B.　The answer is 3 months.

92.　D.　The correct answer is 35 years of age.

93.　D.　The answer is 150% under the Indiana Small Group Statute.

LIFE AND HEALTH PRODUCER
INDIANA EXAMINATION CONTENT OUTLINE
160 QUESTIONS TOTAL
REVISED 7/10/2015

I. INSURANCE BASICS   **(21 QUESTIONS TOTAL)**

    A. The Very Basics   **(3 QUESTIONS)**

        1. What is insurance

        2. Understanding Risk

        3. The Law of Large Numbers

        4. Types of insurance companies
- Lloyd's of London
- Stock companies
- Mutual companies
- Fraternals

        5. Reinsurance

    B. Contract Law   **(12 QUESTIONS)**

        1. What is a contract

        2. The five essential parts of a contract
- Offer
- Acceptance
- Consideration
- Legal capacity
- Legal purpose

        3. Insurance Specifics
- Who makes the offer
- Who accepts the offer
- What is each party's consideration

        4. Defining truth
- Warranties
- Representations
- Misrepresentations
- Concealment
- Material to the risk
- Consequences of material misrepresentation on the application

© 2017 Pathfinder Corporation

5. Insurable Interest

6. Consent

7. When does coverage start
- If no Interim Insuring Agreement is used
- If an Interim Insuring Agreement is used
  o Conditional Receipts
  o Collecting the initial premium

8. Policy delivery
- Agent's responsibilities
- Statement of Continued Good Health

9. Unique characteristics of insurance contracts
- Conditional
- Valued, Reimbursement & Service contracts
- Unilateral
- Adhesion
- Aleatory

10. Other contract terms
- Waiver
- Fraud

11. Insurance law & the Agent/Producer
- The Agent/Producer
- The Agency Agreement/ Contract
- The Agent's extending the insurance company's liability
- Agent's knowledge
- Agent vs. Broker

12. Powers of Agency
- Expressed authority
- Implied authority
- Apparent authority

C. Underwriting Basics (6 QUESTIONS)

1. What is underwriting

2. Why is underwriting necessary

3. Relationship between risk and premiums charged

4. Sources of insurability information
   - Application
     - o Making changes on the application
     - o Consequence of an incomplete application (blanks)
     - o Required signatures on the application
   - Agent/Producer's reports
   - Medical information & medical exams
   - The Medical Information Bureau (MIB) and disclosures
   - Attending Physician's reports
   - Credit reports
     - o Fair Credit Reporting Act & mandatory disclosures
   - Inspection reports

5. Selection & Classification Factors
   - Age
   - Gender (sex)
   - Tobacco usage
   - Occupation
   - Avocation, etc.

6. AIDS, HIV & Underwriting

7. Classification of Risks & Effects on premiums charged
   - Preferred
   - Standard
   - Substandard
   - Declined

8. Gross Premium factors
   - Risk (Mortality and Morbidity)
   - Interest
   - Expense

9. Net Premium

10. Premium Modes
    - Effect on Premiums

II. TYPES OF LIFE INSURANCE POLICIES   (16 QUESTIONS TOTAL)

A. Term Life Insurance   (2-3 QUESTIONS)
1. Level Term
2. Decreasing Term
3. Increasing Term
4. Renewable Term
5. Convertible Term
6. Level Premium Term
7. Maturity
8. Taxation

B. Whole Life Insurance   (3-4 QUESTIONS)
1. Permanent Protection
2. Cash value
   - Guaranteed growth of Cash Value
   - Taxation
   - Policy loans and interest charged
3. Level premium payments
4. Methods of Premium Payment
   - Single Premium
   - Limited-Pay
   - Continuous Premium/Straight Life
5. Maturity
6. Taxation

C. Adjustable Life Insurance   (0-1 QUESTION)
1. Factors that can be adjusted
   - Amount of death protection
   - Amount of premium
   - Type of plan (Term versus Whole Life)
2. Advantages and Disadvantages

D. Variable Whole Life Insurance   **(0-1 QUESTION)**

    1. A securities version of Whole Life insurance

    2. The Separate Investment Account (as opposed to the General Account)

    3. Additional licensing is required to sell securities products
       • National Association of Securities Dealers (NASD)

E. Universal Life Insurance   **(3-4 QUESTIONS)**

    1. Permanent Protection

    2. Policy design and structure

    3. Annual management fees

    4. Death benefit options

    5. Flexible premium options

    6. Cash accumulation options
       • Cash value growth on an interest sensitive basis
       • Tax deferred growth
       • Partial surrenders
       • Tax consequences of partial surrenders
       • Policy loans

    7. Waiver of Premium vs. Waiver of Cost of Insurance

    8. Taxation

F. Variable Universal Life Insurance   **(0-1 QUESTION)**

    1. A securities version of Universal Life insurance

    2. Special securities licensing requirements (NASD)

G. Interest Sensitive Whole Life Insurance   **(0-1 QUESTION)**

H. Equity Indexed Life Insurance   **(1 QUESTION)**

I. Joint Life Insurance   **(0-1 QUESTION)**

    1. Number of Insureds

    2. First to die

J. Survivorship Life Insurance   **(0-1 QUESTION)**

    1. Number of Insureds

    2. Last to die

K. Family (Protection) Policy   (0-1 QUESTION)
1. Policy structure
2. Who are the insureds
3. Newborns and adopted children
4. Premium factors

L. Other Life Insurance Policy Types   (0-1 QUESTION)
1. Modified Life
2. Graded Premium Whole Life
3. Re-Entry Term
4. Juvenile Life
5. Credit Life

M. Modified Endowment Contracts (MEC) (1 QUESTION)
1. IRS Definition/ Seven-Pay test
2. Taxation
3. 10% Penalty for early withdrawal
4. Age 59 ½ Rule

III. ANNUITY CONTRACTS   (7 QUESTIONS TOTAL)

A. Concept of an Annuity

B. The Accumulation (pay-in) Period vs. the Annuity (pay-out/liquidation) Period

C. The Pay-In Period
1. Who controls policy
2. Premium payment options
3. Cash value grows tax deferred
4. Penalty for contract surrender prior to age 59 ½
   • Exceptions
5. May be surrender charges for early withdrawals
6. Tax consequences of policy surrender
7. Consequences of policyowner death during the pay-in period
   • Taxation

© 2017 Pathfinder Corporation

D. The Pay-Out Period

1. Age 59 ½ Rule
2. Choices
   - Take the Money
   - Annuity Certain
   - Life Annuity
3. Annuity Certain
   - Fixed Period
   - Fixed Amount
4. Life Annuity
   - Who controls policy
   - Policyowner becomes the Annuitant
   - Annuitant(s) will receive a life income
   - Annuitant can name a beneficiary should there be any installment payments made after the death of the Annuitant.
   - Exclusion Ratio
   - Pay out choices include:
     - o Straight Life (or Life Only) Annuity
     - o Life Annuity with Period Certain
     - o Refund Life Annuity
     - o Joint and Survivor Life Annuity

E. Types of Annuities

1. Fixed Dollar (Conventional) Annuity-General Account
2. Variable Annuity-Separate Account-NASD license required
3. Equity Indexed Annuity

F. Other Annuity Terms

1. Immediate vs. Deferred Annuity
2. Single Premium vs. Level Premium vs. Flexible Premium payment plans

IV. LIFE INSURANCE POLICY PROVISIONS   (8 QUESTIONS TOTAL)

A. Required Provisions   (5-6 QUESTIONS)

1. Entire Contract/Changes Clause
2. Insuring Clause
3. Premium Payment Clause
4. Incontestable Clause
5. Misstatement of Age and Sex Clause
6. Grace Period Clause
7. Reinstatement Clause
8. Ownership Clause
9. Assignment Clause
10. Loan Values and Automatic Premium Loan (APL) Provision
11. Time Limit on Lawsuits
12. Methods of Settlement
13. The Practice of Back-Dating
14. Application of State Law
15. Free Look Provision

B. Discretionary Provisions (Exclusions)   (0-1 QUESTION)

1. Suicide Clause
2. Hazardous Occupation (or Hobby/Avocation) Clause

C. Beneficiary Designations   (2 QUESTIONS)

1. Policyowner can name and change beneficiary designations
2. Primary and Contingent beneficiaries
3. Revocable and Irrevocable designations
4. The Estate as beneficiary
5. A Trust as beneficiary
6. Minors (children) as beneficiaries
7. Uniform Simultaneous Death Act
   • Common Disaster Provision
8. Naming Beneficiaries
   • Per capita
   • Per stirpes
9. Spendthrift Clause

V. LIFE INSURANCE POLICY OPTIONS   (7 QUESTIONS TOTAL)

A. Dividend Options   (1-2 QUESTIONS)

1. What are Policy Dividends
2. Taxation
3. Options:
   - Cash
   - Reduction of Premium
   - Accumulate at Interest
   - Paid-Up Additions
   - One Year Term
   - Paid-Up Life

B. Nonforfeiture Options (2 QUESTIONS)

1. Purpose
2. Options:
   - Cash
   - Reduced Paid-Up insurance
   - Extended Term insurance
3. Reinstatement

C. Settlement Options   (1-2 QUESTIONS)

1. Maturity
2. Options:
   - Cash
   - Interest
   - Fixed Period (Annuity Certain)
   - Fixed Amount (Annuity Certain)
   - Life Income (Life Annuity)
     o Straight Life (or Life Only) Annuity
     o Life Annuity with Period Certain
     o Refund Life Annuity
     o Joint and Survivor Life Annuity

D. Living Benefit Options   (1-2 QUESTIONS)

1. Accelerated Death Benefits
2. Viatical Settlements

VI. LIFE INSURANCE POLICY RIDERS   (4 QUESTIONS TOTAL)
   A. Multiple Indemnity/Accidental Death rider
   B. Guaranteed Insurability rider
   C. Cost of Living rider
   D. Waiver of Premium rider
   E. Payor Benefit rider
   F. Accelerated Death Benefit rider
   G. Automatic Premium Loan rider

VII. BUSINESS USES OF LIFE INSURANCE   (1 QUESTION TOTAL)
   A. Key Employee Life policies
   B. Buy and Sell Agreements
   C. Split Dollar plans

VIII. QUALIFIED RETIREMENT PLANS   (3 QUESTIONS TOTAL)
   A. Qualified versus Nonqualified plans
   B. Characteristics of qualified plans
   C. Tax treatment of qualified plans and age limitations (59 ½ & 70 ½)

   D. Penalty for premature withdrawals
       1. Exceptions
   E. Defined Contribution plans versus Defined Benefit plans

   F. Common types of Qualified Retirement plans
       1. 401 K plans
       2. 403 B Tax Sheltered Annuities (TSAs) for 501 C corporations
       3. Individual Retirement Accounts (IRAs)
       4. Roth IRAs
       5. Keogh (HR-10) plans
       6. Simplified Employee Pension (SEPs) plans

   G. Plan Roll-Overs

IX. GROUP LIFE INSURANCE   (3 QUESTIONS TOTAL)

A. Group Insurance Concepts

B. Eligible Groups
1. Single Employers
2. Labor Unions
3. Associations
4. Credit Unions
5. Creditors (Credit Life Insurance)
6. Multiple Employer Trusts (METs)
7. Multiple Employer Welfare Arrangements (MEWAs)

C. The Group Contract
1. Master Contract
2. Individual Certificates of Insurance

D. Group Underwriting
1. Experience rating vs. Community rating
2. Reduced Adverse Selection
3. Group Risk Selection
4. Purpose of the Group
5. Eligible Members
6. No discrimination
7. Contributory vs. Non-Contributory
8. Turnover

E. Reduced Administrative Costs

F. Life Conversion Privileges

X. GOVERNMENT INSURANCE - SOCIAL SECURITY
                                         (1 QUESTION TOTAL)

A. Social Security Retirement Income Benefit
1. Who is Eligible for income benefits
2. Currently Insured vs. Fully Insured status
3. Benefits based on Primary Insurance Amount (PIA)
4. Blackout Period

© 2017 Pathfinder Corporation

XI. HEALTH INSURANCE BASICS

(14 QUESTIONS TOTAL)

(6-8 QUESTIONS)

A. Definitions of Key Terms

1. Insuring Clause
2. Consideration Clause
3. Free Look Provision
4. Probationary (Waiting) Periods
5. Elimination Periods
6. Definition of Perils
   - Accident
   - Sickness
   - Activities of Daily Living (ADLs)
7. Deductibles
   - Dollar Deductibles
   - Time Deductibles (Elimination Periods)
8. Policy Renewal Provisions
   - Noncancellable
   - Guaranteed Renewable
   - Conditionally Renewable
   - Optionally Renewable
   - Cancellable
   - Term (Period of Time)
9. Preexisting Conditions
10. Coinsurance
11. Adverse Selection
12. Included/excluded benefits
    - Individual Medical Expense policies
    - Group Major Medical

B. Common Health Insurance Riders   (1-2 QUESTIONS)
1. Impairment Rider
2. Guaranteed Insurability Rider
3. Multiple Indemnity Rider (AD&D)

C. Major Health Insurance Providers   (3-4 QUESTIONS)
1. Stock and Mutual insurance companies
2. Blue Cross and Blue Shield companies
3. Health Maintenance Organizations (HMOs)
4. Preferred Provider Organizations (PPOs)
5. Multiple Employer Trusts (METs)
6. Multiple Employer Welfare Associations (MEWAs)
7. Federal and State Governments
8. Workers Compensation Plans
9. Health Savings Accounts (HSAs)

D. Tax Treatment of Health Benefits   (1-2 QUESTIONS)

E. Occupational vs. Nonoccupational Coverages   (0-1 QUESTION)

XII. DISABILITY INCOME INSURANCE   (4 QUESTIONS TOTAL)

A. Characteristics of Disability Income Policies
1. Who is the insured
2. How are benefits paid
3. How long are benefits paid
4. To whom are benefits paid
5. Triggers for benefit payments
6. Elimination Periods
7. Taxation of Disability Income benefits

B. Underwriting

C. Benefit Limits

D. Definitions of Total Disability
1. Own Occupation
2. Any Occupation
3. Presumptive Total Disability

E. Definitions of "Partial" Disability
1. Partial Disability Benefits
2. Residual Disability Benefits

F. Other Disability Income Provisions
1. Recurrent Disability
2. Waiver of Premium

G. Business Applications of Disability Income Policies
1. Business Overhead Expense policies
2. Key Employee Disability Income Policies
3. Disability Buy-Sell (Business Disability Buyout) policies
4. Group Disability Income policies

XIII. MEDICAL EXPENSE POLICIES   (6 QUESTIONS TOTAL)

A. Characteristics of Medical Expense Policies (2 QUESTIONS)
1. Pays medical bills (doctors, hospitals, drugs, etc.)
2. Insureds
3. Deductibles and coinsurance requirements
4. Probationary (Waiting) periods
5. Taxation
6. Concept of "Managed Care"

B. Types of Plans   (3 QUESTIONS)
1. Basic Plans (Hospital, Medical & Surgical)
2. Major Medical Policy characteristics
   • Catastrophic Coverages
   • Dollar Deductibles
   • Eligible Expenses-Usual, necessary and customary
   • Coinsurance/cost sharing
   • Per Person Maximum Benefit Limits
   • Common Exclusions
   • Calculate a simple Major Medical Claim

C. Medical Expense (1 QUESTION)

1. Assignment of Benefits
2. Rights of Conversion
3. Rights of Newborn and Adopted Children
4. Rights of Dependent Children

XIV. SENIOR CITIZEN POLICIES   (6 QUESTIONS TOTAL)

A. Long Term Care (LTCs) Policies   (2-3 QUESTIONS)

1. Purpose
2. Types of Benefits paid
3. Standard Provisions
4. Minimum Benefit Period
5. Levels of Care
   - Skilled Nursing Care
   - Intermediate Care
   - Custodial or Residential Care
   - Home Health Care
   - Adult Day Care
   - Respite Care
6. LTC Disclosure and Performance Standards
   - Preexisting Condition Limits
   - 30-Day Free Look Provision
   - Outline of Coverages
   - Policy Summary

B. Medicare Supplement Policies (MSPs) (2-3 QUESTIONS)

1. Purpose
2. Eligibility
3. Standard Provisions
4. Required Forms of Renewability
5. Nonduplication of Coverages
6. Probationary Period limits
7. Benefit Limits
8. Twelve Standardized Plans A-L
9. MSP Disclosure and Performance Standards

© 2017 Pathfinder Corporation

C. LTC and MSP Marketing Requirements (0-1 QUESTION)
   1. Suitability
   2. Nonduplication of Coverage
   3. Policy Summaries, Outlines of Coverage & Buyers Guides
   4. Notices Regarding Policy Replacements
   5. Permitted Compensation Arrangements

XV. ACCIDENTAL DEATH AND DISMEMBERMENT (AD&D) POLICIES (1Q)

   A. Conditions For Payment Of The Death Claim (Principal Sum)

   B. Accidental Dismemberment (Capital Sum)

XVI. LIMITED HEALTH POLICIES   (1 QUESTION TOTAL)

   A. Hospital Indemnity policies

   B. Prescription Drug policies

   C. Dread Disease policies

   D. Dental Expense policies

   E. Vision Care policies

XVII. UNIFORM INDIVIDUAL HEALTH POLICY PROVISIONS (8 Q TOTAL)

   A. The Required Provisions
      1. Entire Contract/Changes
      2. Time Limit on Certain Defenses or Incontestable
      3. Grace Period
      4. Reinstatement
      5. Notice of Claim
      6. Claim Forms
      7. Proof of Loss
      8. Time of Payment of Claims
      9. Payment of Claims
      10. Physical Examination and Autopsy
      11. Legal Action
      12. Change of Beneficiary
      13. Relation of Earnings to Insurance: Average Earnings

© 2017 Pathfinder Corporation

B. The Optional Policy Provisions

    1. Change of Occupation

    2. Misstatement of Age

    3. Illegal Occupation

    4. Other Insurance in this Insurer

    5. Insurance with Other Insurers: Expense Incurred Basis

    6. Insurance with Other Insurers: Other Benefits

    7. Unpaid Premium

    8. Cancellation

    9. Conformity with State Statutes

    10. Intoxicants and Narcotics

XVIII. GROUP HEALTH   (6 QUESTIONS TOTAL)

A. Key Concepts

    1. Medical exam requirements

    2. Occupational Losses

    3. Maternity Benefit requirements

    4. Rights of Dependent Children

    5. Preexisting Conditions limitations

    6. Changing insurance companies - no loss/no gain

    7. Coordination of Benefits clause

       • Primary vs. Secondary coverages

       • Simple Claim Problem

B. Portability Issues

    1. COBRA

    2. HIPAA

XIX. GOVERNMENT SOCIAL SECURITY HEALTH CARE (3 Q TOTAL)

A. Medicare Title 18

    1. Eligibility

    2. Four Coverage Parts

       • Automatic Part A Hospital

       • Optional Part B Medical

       • Optional Part C Medicare + Choice

       • Optional Part D Drug Benefit

       • Premium requirements

B. Medicaid Title 19
1. Eligibility
2. Benefits
3. Funding
4. Administration

C. Social Security Disability Income benefits (SSDI)
1. Definition of Total Disability
2. Triggers
3. Duration of benefits
4. Benefits based on your PIA

XX. STATE OF INDIANA
GENERAL INSURANCE REGULATIONS   (24 QUESTIONS TOTAL)

A. Department of Insurance   (6 QUESTIONS)
1. Insurance Commissioner
   • Appointment by Governor
   • Member of NAIC
   • Powers
   • Duties
2. Admission of Insurance Companies
   • Certificate of Authority
   • Admitted versus Non-Admitted companies
   • Domestic, Foreign & Alien companies
3. Examination of Admitted Insurance Companies
   • Frequency of fiscal examinations
   • Waiving examinations of Foreign & Alien companies
5. Insurance Guaranty Associations
   • Purpose
   • Policy benefits that are guaranteed

B. Licensing Laws   (11 QUESTIONS)
1. Types of Insurance Licenses, Eligibility Requirements & Powers and Duties
   • Resident Producer
   • Nonresident Producer
   • Temporary Producer
   • Consultant
   • Limited Lines

  o Travel/Flight
  o Portable Electronics
  o Title
  o Credit
  o Funeral Directors

2. Who must be licensed
- Solicit, negotiate or sell contracts of insurance

3. Producer qualifications and the licensing process

4. Insurance Company: Producer appointments and termination

5. Duties of a Producer
- License application process, examination, and fees for obtaining a license
- Controlled Business
- Acting as a Consultant
- Fees and commissions

6. Producer's License Maintenance
- Producer notification requirements for change of business or residential address
- License renewal process
- Continuing Education requirements
- Sircon license & C/E tracking system
  o Producer Responsibilities

C. Producer/Company Compliance (6 QUESTIONS)

1. Producer Licensing Law & Violations

2. Unfair Competition Law & Violations

3. Definitions
- Twisting
- Rebating
- Sharing commissions with an unlicensed person
- Unfair discrimination

4. Complaint process
- Time frame for hearings

5. Penalties/Disciplinary Actions
- Penalty for violating Licensing law
- Penalty for violating Unfair Competition Law
- Penalty for violating Cease and Desist Orders
- Criminal violations

D. Claims   (1 QUESTION)
    1. When must claims be paid
    2. Unfair Claim Settlement Practices

XXI. LIFE REGULATIONS   (8 QUESTIONS TOTAL)

A. Policies and Contracts   (4 QUESTIONS)
    1. Policy Provisions
    2. Underwriting Restrictions
    3. Right to Examine (10 Day Free Look)
    4. Payment of Claims
    5. Interest on Loans
    6. Interest on Death Benefits
    7. AIDS & HIV
    8. Accelerated Death Benefits
    9. Viatical Settlements

B. Marketing Practices   (3 QUESTIONS)
    1. Advertising
    2. Solicitation
        • Purpose
        • Documentation
        • Buyer's Guide and Policy Summary
        • Duties of Producers
    3. Replacement
        • Definition of Replacement
        • Purpose
        • Free Look
        • Duties of Producers
        • Duties of Companies

C. Group Life   (1 QUESTION)
    1. Eligible Groups
    2. Conversion Rights to Individual Policy

© 2017 Pathfinder Corporation

XXII. HEALTH REGULATIONS (8 QUESTIONS TOTAL)

A. Health Insurance Contracts   (3 QUESTIONS)
1. Standard Provisions in Medical Expense and Disability Income Policies
    - Individual Provisions
    - Group Provisions
2. Required Coverages
    - Mammogram coverage
3. Underwriting Restrictions
4. Rights of Dependent Children
    - Newborns and adopted children
    - Limiting age
    - Handicapped children
    - Adopted children
5. Advertising

B. Specialized Coverage   (2 QUESTIONS)
1. Indiana Comprehensive Health Insurance Association (ICHIA)
2. Indiana Small Group Health
3. Group Coordination of Benefits
4. Children's Health Insurance Program (CHIP)

C. Long Term Care and Medicare Supplement Policies   (3 QUESTIONS)
1. Provisions
    - Free Look
    - Length of coverage
    - Pre-existing conditions, etc.
2. Standards for Marketing
3. Replacement
4. Producer's Duties
5. Long Term Care Partnership Program (LTCP)

END